Making Sense as a School Leader

Richard H. Ackerman
Gordon A. Donaldson Jr.
Rebecca van der Bogert

Foreword by Roland S. Barth

Making Sense as a School Leader

Persisting Questions, Creative Opportunities

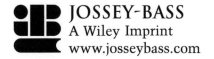

JOSSEY-BASS
A Wiley Imprint
www.josseybass.com

Published by Jossey-Bass
A Wiley Imprint
989 Market Street, San Francisco, CA 94103-1741   www.josseybass.com

Jossey-Bass books and products are available through most bookstores. To contact Jossey-Bass directly call our Customer Care Department within the U.S. at 800-956-7739, outside the U.S. at 317-572-3986 or fax 317-572-4002.

Jossey-Bass also publishes its books in a variety of electronic formats. Some content that appears in print may not be available in electronic books.

Library of Congress Cataloging-in-Publication Data

Ackerman, Richard, date.
    Making sense as a school leader : persisting questions, creative opportunities / Richard Ackerman, Gordan Donaldson, Jr., Rebecca van der Bogert. — 1st ed.
        p.   cm. — (The Jossey-Bass education series)
    Includes bibliographical references (p.   ) and index.
    ISBN 0-7879-0164-4 (alk. paper)
    1. School principals—United States.   2. Educational leadership— United States.   3. School management and organization—United States.   I. Donaldson, Gordon A., Jr.   II. Van der Bogert, Rebecca. III. Title.   IV. Series.
LB2831.92.A28   1996
371.2'012'0973—dc20   95-37019

Printed in the United States of America
FIRST EDITION
HB Printing   10 9

The Jossey-Bass Education Series

Contents

Foreword

The volume you are about to engage stands out from a sea of pedestrian homogenized literature about the development of school leaders. Many qualities make this a distinctive and a distinguished piece of work.

It is demanding: not in the usual sense of placing upon the reader the burden to figure out what the writer is saying. To the contrary, I find the style and content remarkably accessible. This book demands that the aspiring and practicing principal forgo the very understandable need to fix, once and for all, the nagging problems of the school so that one may get on with the more important business of leadership. The seven doggedly persistent tensions which constitute the organizing principle of this book will never be "fixed," because the search for a quick fix to complexity is, of course, illusory. The gift of the book is that it helps us to acknowledge undeniably these tensions, to begin to reflect seriously upon them, and then to commit to the continuous inventive struggle to live successfully within them. This, I find, is *precisely* the important business of school leadership.

The seven tensions ring true in my experience as a school principal in the sixties and seventies. They accurately characterize the difficulties principals reported when I worked at the Harvard Principals' Center in the eighties. I suspect they will speak forcefully to your experiences in the nineties—even if you have not yet had them. They are, in fact, the tensions that come with the territory of school leadership, whether it be public or private; rural, urban, or suburban; elementary, middle, or high school.

That the authors have fastened onto such generic issues is note-worthy. What they do with them and how they do it is equally dis-tinctive. Imaginatively employing the emerging art form of case stories, they bring these enduring tensions to life with the very real faces of teachers, parents, students, members of the central office, and of course, principals themselves.

By putting themselves onto their own stage as actors as well as producers, they inject authenticity, controversy, humor, credibility, and above all, craft wisdom from their own collective years of school leadership. These are not simply scholars writing about the work you should do: they are colleagues writing in a thoughtful way about the work they should have done and now would like to do, thereby ensuring that the insights they have gleaned from the craft will be available to others. All too little of this craft knowledge is available in our profession. What is also unusual, and for me a relief, is the absence of abstract models, theories, flow charts, idealized job descriptions, and preachy prescriptions. The real world in the cor-ridors of P.S. 96 at 8:10 in the morning doesn't work like that.

Finally, what makes this a distinctive and distinguished piece of literature on school leadership in my library is the very ambitious, risky, and adventuresome attempt by the authors to *model* their mes-sage. Given the constraints of the printed page, I find this coura-geous indeed. To paraphrase Ralph Waldo Emerson, "What we do speaks so loudly that no one can hear what we say." What these authors do here both complements and amplifies what they say. The result is a most powerful effort.

You will be exhorted, as a school leader, to take risks with new forms. The authors have taken enormous risks here. They want you to engage with your school community in a continuing conversa-tion about good schools. They take part, before our eyes, in a con-tinuing dialogue about the important issues of school leadership. They urge you to disclose, to be vulnerable, to put it out there. They do. They ask you to trust in and to be respectful of the strength, wis-dom, and ability of your school colleagues. You will find that they trust in you and are indeed respectful of your strengths, wisdom, and ability—as they are of one another. They challenge you not to go it alone but to share leadership and decision making with others. They do. They urge you to share your craft knowledge. They do. They urge you to honor diversity in all of its perplexing forms. They do. They counsel us not to look for simplicity but to live hospitably with the complexity of important tensions. They do. Above all, they impress upon us that most important quality of school leadership: being a lifelong, voracious, and visible learner, and thereby a leader. This volume and the many-year exercise of writing it together has been a profoundly personal and professional, and now visible, learning experience for each of its authors.

So dear reader, enjoy, as I have, struggling with, celebrating, and above all, learning from this lively little cruise through the seas of school leadership on which you are about to embark.

August 1995   ROLAND S. BARTH

Welcome to Our Readers

You are about to join a conversation that the three of us have been pursuing for at least a dozen years. It is about what principals do, what they think about, and what they value as they work to help their schools to thrive.

As you will see, our work as principals and our discussions with each other have taught us that school leadership is neither finite nor static. It is not something that can be mastered once and for all, nor is it a particular set of skills that can readily be acquired. Rather, school leadership is a quest to shape a complex, dynamic, exciting entity called a school into a place not only where all children acquire valuable knowledge and skills but also where children and adults alike are valued, respected, and challenged to be their best. Like schools themselves, leadership is dynamic; it bubbles with uncertainty and requires immense discretion and attentiveness. Our collective experience in the professional development of school leaders has taught us that leadership work is never done.

We have written this book as a way of bringing others into our quest to make sense of the principal's leadership work. The journey from conversation to book has not been easy. Books are finite. They lend themselves to definitive pronouncements. Books generally have neither the give-and-take of our conversations nor the excitement that accompanies sense making. Books often make readers feel as if their own knowledge plays second fiddle to the knowledge contained in the book. We don't believe that to be true. We have organized our book around questions, and we have structured the chapters conversationally, around principals' case stories.

During our work, we have kept a variety of readers in mind. Foremost for us are practicing and aspiring principals. Our fondest image is of a group of principals and potential principals using our book to ignite lively and productive conversations among themselves about their own leadership in their schools. We hope, as well, that our question-centered approach to school leadership will enhance the way some school superintendents, central office personnel, professors, and professional developers support, supervise, and prepare principals. Our conversation has been thought-provoking for us. In sharing it, our goal is to provoke new thought and energy among and about principals.

As three former principals with faith in the leadership potential of principals, we have focused our conversations on the need to clarify our own work, the work of our colleagues, and the chemistry within schools as it affects the learning of students. Throughout these conversations, we have coaxed and prodded and pushed each other to think beyond our comfort levels, to see old problems we had faced as school leaders in a new light, and to discover—with the inspiration of that light—some new solutions to those old problems. Although Becky has become a superintendent in Winnetka, Illinois; Richard, a professor in Massachusetts; and Gordy, a professor in Maine, we remain involved in the work of principals and their schools. Our conversation—as well as our own leadership quests—continues.

We hope you find our conversation easy to enter. You will see that we provide fewer "answers" than many books about principals. We have sought to guide you to understanding and examining your own thoughts, feelings, and recurring questions concerning principals' work. We hope that in doing so, you will see your work, your school, and yourself in a new light.

In the spirit of true conversation, we invite you to correspond with us. We urge you to use our book to spawn conversations among your colleagues; within your schools, colleges, and companies; and with yourself. We are anxious to learn what your leadership quest is teaching you and how your leadership has helped children and adults as learners. Please write us.

Welcome to our conversation!

Becky, Gordy, and Richard
International Network of Principals' Centers
Principals' Center at Harvard University
Harvard Graduate School of Education
336 Gutman Library
Cambridge, Mass. 02138

Acknowledgments

Making Sense as a School Leader comes from good conversations among ourselves and many others. Our book reflects the collective development of a series of ideas on school leadership, as well as the genuine friendships that have emerged through the sharing of these ideas. Our collaboration has not been so much a philosophical or ideological compact. Rather, it has been the experience of carefully and honestly talking and listening with each other over the course of many years, examining common problems of school leadership that we each care about, and supporting one another in doing something about them.

This experience of leadership sense-making has made friends of us all. We dedicate this book to those who have joined us in this journey. To our fellow principals, students, teachers, professors, superintendents, members of the International Network of Principals' Centers, friends, and family, we thank you.

Collectively we'd like to give special acknowledgment to Roland Barth, Joe Richardson, Milli Blackman, and David Hagstrom for being such a significant part of our conversations. Individually we each have others to whom we are grateful. Richard is deeply indebted to Carla Beebe for seeing the important questions in the questions, to university colleagues Robert Gower, Norman Benson, Chuck Christensen, Judy Boccia, Don Pierson, Joyce Gibson, John LeBaron, Clarence Tolbert, and Lee Teitel for affirming the questions, to members of Lowell Leadership Academy and all his students at University of Massachusetts Lowell and Harvard Graduate School of Education for living them. Gordy thanks Cynthia, Morgaen, Cary, Nell, and Ben for enduring the hours on the keyboard and the phone, and George Marnik, Dave Brown, and members of the Maine Academy for School Leaders for their collegial inspiration. Becky is forever grateful to Giles, Bo, Johann, Art, Aril, Dini, Kirby, her father, and Ma vdB for being the wind beneath her wings, to her colleagues of the Winthrop School for teaching her the spirit of shared leadership, to Marcia Adelman for joining in the conversation of this manuscript with a careful eye and thoughtful heart, to Ilene for everything, and to her colleagues in Winnetka for the meaningful conversations of this year and the many more to come.

And of course we are grateful for the rich dialogue and deep friendship that has grown among the three of us. We couldn't have done it without each other!

The Authors

Richard H. Ackerman is assistant professor of education at the University of Massachusetts, Lowell College of Education and lecturer on education at the Harvard Graduate School of Education. He earned his master of science in education (1982) at the Bank Street College and both his master of arts (1985) and doctorate in education (1989) at the Harvard University, Graduate School of Education. Before joining the staff at Lowell and Harvard, Ackerman was an elementary school teacher and an administrator.

He draws primary inspiration from his teaching and his work with practicing principals. For the past five years, Ackerman has served as the co-director of the International Network of Principals' Centers, which was established to foster the exchange of ideas and to facilitate professional communication among principals' centers and leadership academies in the United States and worldwide.

Ackerman's research has focused on leadership development, experiential education, school reform, and the development of case studies and stories for teaching educational administration.

Gordon A. Donaldson Jr. is professor of education at the University of Maine and coordinator of the Maine Network of School Leaders. He earned his bachelor of arts in Russian history (1967) from Harvard College. While teaching in Philadelphia, Boston, and North Haven, Maine, he earned a master of arts in teaching (1970) and a doctorate in education (1976) from Harvard University.

Donaldson's years as the principal of an eight-hundred-student grades–seven-to-twelve school in Ellsworth, Maine, became the touchstone of his first book, *Learning to Lead: The Dynamics of the High School Principalship* (1991). His active involvement in professional development for principals encompasses his experience as a principal and his tenure as a professor. Donaldson cofounded one of the first principals' academies in the country in 1979, was a founding member of the International Network of Principals' Centers, directed the Maine Academy for School Leaders, and has served on several committees of the National Association of Secondary School Principals.

Donaldson has written widely about school leadership, particularly the professional development of school leaders. *Becoming Better Leaders: The Challenge of Improving Student Learning* (1995) and *As Leaders Learn: Personal Stories of Growth in School Leadership* (1995) were coauthored and co-edited respectively with George Marnik, a practicing Maine principal.

Maine's landscape, schools, people, the Donaldson family, and an old farm are the sources of vitality and insight for his writing, teaching, and leadership in professional development.

Rebecca van der Bogert is superintendent of schools in Winnetka, Illinois, and founding member and co-director of the International Network of Principals' Centers at Harvard University. She earned her bachelor of arts in psychology (1967) and her master of science in special education (1968) from Syracuse University and her doctorate in education (1991) from Harvard University, Graduate School of Education. While at Harvard she served on the Editorial Board of the *Harvard Educational Review* and is currently serving on the Harvard Graduate School of Education Alumni Council.

At the heart of van der Bogert's work in public schools has been her commitment to the importance of the relationships between people within both the school and the community. She has served as classroom teacher, guidance counselor, resource teacher, coordinator of a gifted and talented program, principal, assistant superintendent, director of curriculum, university instructor, and superintendent of schools. In all these capacities she has engaged in the study and practice of shared decision making and the nurturing of an environment in which all concerned are respected and valued for their contributions and encouraged to grow.

Van der Bogert has shared her experiences with others through extensive writing, editing, speaking, and consulting with numerous school systems and organizations.

Making Sense as a School Leader

Chapter One

Leadership as Quest

Books about the principalship remind us of the story about the blindfolded people and the elephant. Each person describes the part of the elephant he or she touches. Because none of them feels the same part, their individual perceptions of the elephant differ. Similarly, books about principals focus only on parts of principals' work—technical aspects, legal aspects, moral issues, or staff relationships. We hope our book will add a fresh perspective to this melange, one that is closer to the core of principal leadership.

We think of principals as *sense makers* for their schools. Their success at leading hinges, to a great degree, on their ability to see clearly the school's core functions, to evaluate events in light of those functions, and to help the members of the school community conduct their work and their relationships in ways that serve these core functions. This is the task for many of our readers: to make sense of the kaleidoscopic nature of principals' work so that they can understand how their energies and talents can most effectively benefit children's learning. This book shares some of the sense that practicing principals have made of their own complex work. More important, it invites you to join us and others in sense making for your own role and for your school.

Conversations among the three of us and with colleagues have taught us that true leadership has no formula. It is the product of a chemistry between person, staff, students, and the community. It requires constant thought, observation, people skills, judgment, trust, and humor. We have learned that these qualities are neither finite nor quantifiable. You cannot acquire them once and for all. Even good principals never have enough of them.

We have come to see leadership as a quest. We have been frustrated by thinking, What must I learn *to do* to be an effective principal? as if one could somehow ingest enough learning before starting the job. We were never able to predict all the situations and types of people we had to deal with, nor could we anticipate the many problems and joys we experienced as principals. We grew tired and suspicious of thinking there was one "tool box" of strategies that we needed to acquire and to master to make it as principals. Instead, we have found comfort and fulfillment in viewing leadership as a process—as learning to be a principal. It is a perpetual process that entails learning to think and act as a leader, in response to the ever-changing challenges of learning and dealing with growing children and the adults who care about them.

For us, viewing leadership as a quest has had a liberating effect. The leader in quest envisions purposes, asks questions, seeks answers, and enlists others in the quest. Principals need to ask continually if the school's work fulfills its basic purposes and mission. As principals receive new challenges, they need to seek specific remedies that fit each challenge, each child, each situation. Their responses need to entrust and empower others—teachers, parents, and children—to take action for the children's sake. Principals' learning is continuous, just as the learning of teachers and students must be.

This realization has led us to structure our book's conversation around seven persisting questions that, we believe, are at the core of principals' work. The quest for optimal learning for all children has led us and many other principals to these seven questions over and over again. These questions reflect the tensions that are inherent in principals' work, tensions that are nested within the varied and sometimes competing interests and activities of schools. These tensions are predictable and can be expected in any principalship. Our own growth as principals and educators has benefited deeply from ongoing exploration into these questions and into what they imply we should do as leaders.

Our book introduces you to these persisting questions and seeks to engage you (and others you wish to join you) in examining your own knowledge base, your beliefs and values, and your talents, skills, and behaviors in working with others. We have gained greatly from exploring the effects of these central leadership issues and discovering how our own talents and limitations affect our actions. Thinking about these issues out loud, along with colleagues, has made the quest both more successful and immensely less lonely.

Why Structure Leadership Learning Around Persisting Questions?

In our work, we have found that leaders who embrace open inquiry, the sharing of problems and solutions, and collective responsibility will foster creativity, resourcefulness, and collaboration in the work of staff and the learning of children. These characteristics are the earmarks of leaders who seek to learn and to invent through questioning. Notice we do not say that leaders *get* the answers to the questions. As many current writers argue (Senge, 1990a; Bennis and Nanus, 1985; Bridges, 1992; Fullan and Hargreaves, 1991), effective leadership has more to do with understanding and then harnessing the dynamics of an organization than it does with imposing answers and structures on it. We see successful principals the same as Bridges (1992), Joyce (1990), and McPherson, Crowson, and Pitner (1986) do: they are problem solvers, decision makers, vision seekers, and relationship builders with and for their school communities. For people who must succeed in these activities, it is often more important to know what questions to ask and how to enlist others in solutions than it is to impose an answer.

We think this question-centered approach is relevant and necessary for schools for three basic reasons. First, schools are neither static nor predictable organizations, nor do they have a single, dependable "technology" for teaching children effectively. Each year a new batch of children and parents will present new challenges and tensions to principals and staffs. Each child, family, and learning or behavior problem is a bit different from all others. Yet they are all variations on basic themes in education, human development, and ethics. The persisting questions in this book embody these basic themes. They involve the toughest issues for any human institution or community: for example, ensuring respect for all, seeing that limited resources are allocated in the wisest way, and judging the quality of a person's performance.

While these issues may seem old to a principal and even to a prospective principal, the particulars of them and the best solutions to them are unique and important to each child and each parent as they experience them. Each day, principals encounter new versions of these old challenges. We suggest that rather than approaching the principalship as if they could resolve the tough discipline, supervision, and goal-setting questions once and for all, principals will find it far healthier and more productive to accept the persistence of these questions and to understand how vitally important each one is to the people involved. Our approach encourages principals to honor and respect each new child, each parent, and the school staff who must work together to do what is right for that child's education. Their work will generate tensions for them and for the principal. The persisting questions in this book lie at the heart of recognizing and dealing with these tensions.

A second reason this question-centered approach makes sense to us is that it views leadership as a learning activity; it allows us to see leaders as learners. This approach not only fits our image of the work principals do, but it presents principals as model learners for others. Principals who are *lead learners* are adults who relish questions and the pursuit of deeper understanding. Their primary focus is the work the adults are engaged in with the children in their schools. Their professional lives center around the goals, programs, and experiences relevant to the learning of both adults and children and on collecting and using evidence of their own success as learners to enhance their performance as leaders.

This picture is neither orderly nor predictable. It looks and feels more like a bubbling stew than a smooth-running machine. Most of the "business" that surfaces from this bubbling pot—especially for the principal—comes in the form of questions, problems, and requests that cannot be answered, resolved, or fulfilled by parents, kids, teachers, coaches, counselors, or anyone else. As any principal knows, these events are more numerous, more varied, and more unruly than any single person can handle. The principal, then, is thrust into collaborative problem solving: questioning others to facilitate their own question answering and seeking solutions collaboratively. The image is one of a public learner. In our own work in schools, we have seen how powerful a model the principal's public learning can be for students, staff, and ordinary citizens (Barth, 1990; Donaldson, 1991; Carmichael, 1981). Put simply, if children are to be inquisitive, resourceful, energetic, and responsible for their own learning and behavior, so must every adult in the school, and most especially—so must the principal.

Finally, we have taken a question-centered approach because it works. The three of us have experienced its benefits and have witnessed its power in many others. Each of us is well schooled in the old paradigm: we have read the textbooks, taught the textbooks, referred to the textbooks in our practices. We have participated in professional and in-service activities that were more answer-centered than question-centered. But we have also been participants in innovative approaches to principal learning and professional development (see Appendix A).

We have each helped pioneer principals' centers and practice-centered approaches to leadership growth in districts and in graduate schools. The common feature of these efforts is their respectful treatment of principals and prospective principals as learners, as agents of their own development. This trust in principals has spawned, in turn, the energetic and sustained participation of those learners in their own improvement as leaders (Donaldson and Marnik, 1995a; "Reflections," 1984–1995). Indeed, the evidence of success is spreading each year as new principal centers start up around the world and as graduate programs in educational administration restructure (Milstein, 1993; Osterman and Kottkamp, 1993). We offer a question-centered approach to leadership development because, in the words of one Maine principal:

> I am more at ease with the process of private reflection than I thought I would be, and my journals have taken on a greater depth of analysis and have increased in both volume and frequency over the last couple of years. I think of all these things as the aftereffects of my involvement with [a one-and-a-half-year question-centered professional development experience].
>
> While significant to me, these are not the effects that are significant to my school. Somehow the style of reflective and cooperative leadership that managed to find its way into my professional person has found its way into my staff. . . . It is my sense that this process is a sort of domino effect [Don Buckingham, personal communication].

Our hope is for this book to start or accelerate a similar domino effect for you, your staff, your students, and your community.

The Seven Persisting Questions

We have identified the seven central questions primarily through reflection on our own work as principals and on the work of other principals. We asked, What are the persisting tensions in principals' work? As we taught classes, led workshops, and grew professionally, we found in others' experiences and in the literature some confirmation of the centrality of these tensions. At the same time, we recognized that others might have an eighth or ninth tension or might take issue with several of ours. That could only make for lively and valuable conversation for us and for you!

Our seven persisting questions stem from these seemingly unresolvable tensions. Irreconcilable conditions and purposes frequently coexist within the context of a school. We believe these qualities are inherent to all schools. The questions arise as much from the fabric of our democracy as from the challenges of educating children en masse. That is why principals are destined to encounter these questions so frequently in their work. It is also why we believe that embracing them and using them to ignite creativity and collaboration makes so much sense.

These are the seven persisting questions:

1. *The Justice Question:* How can we be just to each child, as an individual and as a learner, and create a just and disciplined school as well?

2. *The Teaching Question:* How can we assure our children and the community that every staff member is performing effectively and value each individual staff member as well?

3. *The Purpose Question:* How can we produce measurable learning products and develop children who are capable of healthy learning, social, moral, and work processes as well?

4. *The Resource Question:* How can we encourage constant growth and improvement in our school and acknowledge the realistic limitations on our ability to meet such goals as well?

5. *The Change Question:* How can we foster improvement and change, and respect and value each staff member and citizen as well?

6. *The Ownership Question:* How can we honor the perspectives and purposes of multiple constituencies and work toward unified goals that will benefit all children as well?

7. *The Autonomy Question:* How can we honor teacher creativity and autonomy and share purposes, curricula, and equitable resources as well?

A word of caution: the recurring tensions that give rise to these questions can easily seduce us into either-or thinking. With the Autonomy Question, for example, we often think that the right answer lies either with honoring teacher creativity and autonomy *or* with requiring shared purposes, curriculum, and resources. We believe this is a dangerous course. Our book is about seeing these competing needs as productive partners. The constant challenge to do *both-and* rather than *either-or* gives people in growing schools their verve, their creativity, and their belief in themselves as learners.

Clearly, answers to these persisting questions are difficult to come by. Our intention is not to answer them but to guide your conversations and your thinking toward ideas, perspectives, and resources that will help you to handle them productively in your own work. In doing this, we suggest that you keep in mind two broad domains of knowledge that stream together in the principal's daily work.

The first domain is: what you know about learning, teaching, and organizing an educational institution. In this domain we include, quite literally, what you know to be true about schooling, including factual information, theories you subscribe to, and equally important, beliefs you hold about what works and does not work. For most of us these facts and beliefs are indistinguishable from each other as we use them in leadership. Our discussion of the seven questions is structured to show why and how principals' technical knowledge and beliefs come into play in the solution of problems and in leadership decisions.

Knowledge in the technical domain is necessary but, by itself, insufficient for effective leadership. It is the principal's knowledge and skill in the second or interpersonal domain that is essential to a school's success.

The second domain is the interpersonal relationships and activities essential to effective leadership. Our conversation will lead you to reflect on two varieties of relationships: with one other person— teacher, student, parent, superintendent, secretary; and with a group—a committee, the faculty, the PTA, the entire school as a community. We hope you will explore how you work with other people and perhaps seek feedback about this essential domain. If you are able to read our book in tandem with a colleague or two, you'll be able to share insights about your interpersonal styles and challenges as you ponder how you would respond to these tensions in your own schools.

In both domains we leave to you the specifics as to what you need to learn. We find each principal works in a relatively unique environment. You need to find your own facts, those most pertinent to your needs, before you can knowledgeably attack a challenge. We hope you will find help in the technical domain in the books and other resources we suggest. In Appendix B we offer a framework for assessing your leadership capacities in both domains. We suspect that your greatest growth will result from your own reflection and from regular and honest conversation with others interested in school leadership and in collaboration on your joint search for better strategies. For the three of us, no other learning medium has matched the colleague-critic conversation for deepening our understanding of leadership and our capacities to lead in our own schools. For a quest that promises to last your entire career as a school leader, you'll find no substitute for supportive yet challenging fellow travelers.

The Structure and Spirit of Our Book

Our goal is to make this book a conversation—a dialogue in which participants have equal status and equal responsibility; its purpose is mutual learning. While books are not ideally suited to the give and take of conversations, the concept of the conversation captures the spirit of the book. Having tried systematically to make it reflect our own conversations, we offer it in the hope that it will stimulate yours.

Principals' capacities to make sense of their schools, so they can enlist others gainfully to work for the benefit of children, are important to many people. We hope that teachers, parents, central office personnel, and staff developers will find this approach a useful vehicle for understanding and helping to support principals and other school leaders. But principals themselves are our major audience, those we primarily imagine as participants in our conversation. We especially picture new principals, soon-to-be principals, and principals who are growing weary in the long slog toward school improvement. We hope that whether you read this on your own, in a professional group or graduate course, with a principal colleague or two, or with some of your faculty, you will discover ways to articulate what is happening in your school. Most important, we hope you will gain a better understanding of your role as a leader and will move toward habits of the mind and heart that will make you more effective in that role.

The structure of the book: Chapters Two through Eight present the seven persisting questions and start a developmental conversation about them. In each chapter, we illustrate the question through a case story taken from our own or from other principals' experiences. We provide factual detail to give you a concrete image of the tensions it represents. Each case story is presented through the eyes, ears, and voice of a principal to give access to his or her thoughts, feelings, beliefs, and aspirations. We hope you will see in these case stories parallels to your own school and your own leadership challenges.

Following each case story, we three engage in a conversation about what the principal might do and—equally important—why: that is, we try to make sense of the tension by pursuing answers to the persisting question. One of us offers, through a letter, an analysis of the situation and presents a typical logic for handling it. Another of us responds to the first perspective and offers another approach. We then provide an integrative summary of the prominent issues raised by the story and the two letters, pointing readers toward avenues for making their own sense.

We faced a dilemma as we wrote these seven core chapters: we wanted the conversation in our exchange of letters to be authentic, but we wanted it as well to highlight conflicting viewpoints. In several cases, however, our true personal viewpoints did not substantially conflict. We resolved this dilemma by adhering to our goal as authors: to present true-to-life perspectives of principals that demonstrate major differences in approaching each tension. This meant, in some letters, that we have signed our names as individuals to perspectives that do not truly represent our personal beliefs. We hasten to add, however, that each letter presents a view that is held by—and can be defended by—many principals.

Chapters Nine and Ten address the two central contexts for school leadership: the school as a community and the individual who seeks to lead it. In Chapter Nine, we examine a theme that runs through all seven persisting questions: the principal's ability to help the school function as a community of commitment. We offer suggestions for creating stronger community habits in and around schools. Chapter Ten takes a more personal view of the principal's challenges as raised through the seven questions. We offer five suggestions that have helped us develop faith in ourselves and in others as leaders.

We close with a letter to our readers. It is our epiphany as writers and colleague-critics in this journey toward better school leadership. It centers on us as people with other lives and other attachments beyond our schools. We reflect on the incredible commitments that principals make to their work and on how such dedication taxes them personally in very telling ways. You may want to read the letter before you move on to Chapter Two.

We know many principals who entered the principalship only to be shocked by how different the work was from teaching or counseling or coaching. The sorts of questions we raise had not occurred to them until *after* they had taken the job. We hope this book will encourage you to examine the match between the role of principal and your personal circumstances *before* you apply for or take a position. We hope that if you are currently a principal, you will find ways to achieve a better fit for yourself in your current role or find your way toward another role or another school where the fit is better.

Leadership should not be undertaken blindly or lightly. Our schools need principals who not only aspire to move their schools ahead but also have the background and the capacities to make sense of their dynamic organizations and to share that sense with the school community so that its efforts will be profitably directed. Our own conversations about the central recurring questions of school leadership have helped us immeasurably in the development of our own capacities to think, to be sensitive to others, and to know ourselves as leaders and as people. We hope they do the same for you and your conversations.

Chapter Two

Justice

Doing What's Right . . . But What Is Right?

Principals have been embroiled in student discipline since the role of principal was invented roughly a century ago. No other leadership function is more universally associated with principals than monitoring and shaping the behavior of students. Indeed, we know of few principals whose days do not include conversations with students, teachers, counselors, and parents about how students have behaved and what can be done about it.

Students' behavior—or more accurately their misbehavior—lies at the root of our first persisting question: *how can we treat every student justly when to do so may violate our institutional rules and norms?* Ironically, the question stems from principals' caring about kids. Often, our understanding of what is best for individual kids leads to individualizing our treatment of them. But once we've done that, we hear from colleagues, other students, and parents that what we've done for that child is unfair or preferential treatment over others. Soon we hear that our decisions are inconsistent, that they're leading to chaos and anarchy in the school among both students and staff.

We invite you to experience this persisting question by listening in on Gerry Taylor's case story. Gerry is a young principal at Southside Elementary School, in a changing urban neighborhood. Her story recounts a single disciplinary incident with Sandy, a fifth grader, that is typical of many incidents principals face in school every day. Gerry's attempts to be fair to all parties and to the school community as a whole reveal tensions that, we think, are experienced by all principals. They are tensions between enforcing the rules and caring for each child, between doing what is right for the majority and doing what is right for each child.

Thursday, October 17

Tears streaked down his dusty cheeks, dripping brown on his stained T-shirt. Sandy bordered on hysteria: "She did it! I know she did it! And I'm glad I beat up her jerk-of-a-brother. I see him again, I'm gonna do it again!"

I was beyond words. I'd brought Sandy into my office to contain his abusive language and public anger. It had taken a firm grasp on his arm to get him here. I'd tried calmly talking to him, but his tirade carried on. I'd even tried shouting at him face to face. Nothing calmed him down, so I just waited for his adrenaline to subside.

As I sat there, I tried to piece together what had happened. Frannie Brooks had burst into my office ten minutes earlier. "Come quick," she'd shouted, "there's a fight on the playground!" I dropped everything and dashed down to the recess area. Sandy and Paul were rolling around in the dirt. Sandy had the upper hand; he had Paul by the shirt collar, and was shoving Paul's head into the ground, shrieking at him. I grabbed Sandy under the arms and hauled him off the bleeding Paul.

Frannie looked after Paul; Mrs. Delano dispersed the crowd of onlookers, and I tried to restrain Sandy, who continued to flail about, screaming at Paul. The best I could do was keep him trapped in a corner of the cyclone fence, so he couldn't go after Paul or Paul's sister, Jeanette. After a few minutes of this, Sandy's rage showed little sign of abating. I grasped him by the forearm and marched him to my office.

It took awhile for Sandy's anger to subside. Eventually, he quieted down, sobbing and muttering about how "I hate this place. . . . Nobody don't give me no breaks at this dumb ol' school. . . . How come it's always me that gets hauled in here? How come you don't take that Jeanette and Dawna and Starr and bring them in here? They can't do nothin' wrong, can they?"

At Southside Elementary School, incidents like this happen a couple of times a week. They seem to start with frictions that kids bring to school with them, frictions that kids have anywhere. Southside kids like Sandy have so little adult supervision outside of school that they seem to have more peer problems than most. We end up having to teach them about getting along with others because all they know is the code of the streets.

Southside's neighborhood started changing about five years ago. The number of incidents of this kind is soaring. Paul and his sister Jeanette grew up in Southside. Jeanette's in the fifth grade; Paul, in the sixth. They live with their parents and two smaller siblings three blocks east of school. Sandy arrived last fall, part of a new wave of families that settled in the city when four new plants opened two years ago. Sandy lives with his mother and two older sisters in a housing project four blocks west of Southside. We're witnessing growing tensions between the kids who grew up here and the newcomer kids, usually poorer and more culturally diverse.

The Facts, Please, Just the Facts . . .

10:35: Fifteen minutes after bringing him into the office, I finally felt Sandy was ready to talk about what had happened. I usually try to get a student to discuss what happened, to hear the facts as the student sees them and as others see them. Then I try to figure out who was responsible for what. But in these circumstances, it wouldn't be easy to get the facts. With fights, emotions run high; nobody, including bystanders young and old, sees the facts clearly. Facts, in situations like these, are rarely cold and objective; they're subjective and emotionally charged, the result of comments made between kids and the innuendos of their glances at one another. It's all about who talked with whom, or who allowed whom to play in their recess games: important stuff for them but sometimes difficult for adults to decipher.

That's just how it happened in the case of Sandy, Paul, and Jeanette. As Sandy told it over the next twenty minutes, Jeanette, who was in his fifth grade class, and several of her girlfriends "never leave me alone." He described how, since his arrival seven months ago, they'd called him names, made fun of how he walked and dressed, and "told everybody to give me a hard time." At recess, Sandy had tried to join in Jeanette's brother Paul's game of wall-ball. He'd waited his turn to challenge the winner, but when he stepped forward, Paul told him to "butt out." "So I told him to kiss my ass," Sandy reported, "and he jumped me." As Sandy saw it, "I gave that no-good jerk what he had comin', and his sister and those stupid girls too." According to Sandy, Jeanette had put Paul up to provoking the incident. She was the real target of his anger.

I left Sandy under the watchful eye of Gladys, our school secretary, and began the all-too-familiar routine of collecting facts. After Ms. Brooks had cleaned up his bloody nose, Paul told a different story. He and his sixth-grade buddies were just playing wall-ball, "mindin' our own business when that creep said it was his turn to play the winner." Paul said Sandy grabbed the ball "and wouldn't let us have it." Sandy then threw the ball in Paul's face and "attacked me right there. He just flipped out and came at me. Man, he tore my shirt all up. He was punchin' at me. He's crazy! He oughtta go back where he came from." Paul considered Sandy to be "dead meat." The rules of the playground were one thing, but according to the rules of the neighborhood, Sandy was going to pay for humiliating and hurting Paul.

I was curious about the girls and their part in these events. Did the incident really start with Jeanette and perhaps Dawna and Starr, as Sandy had said? I talked to Dawna and Starr. They pinned the blame entirely on Sandy, though they didn't answer my questions about exactly what had happened with many facts. They echoed a consensus: "That Sandy, he's not right in the head. He just went after Paul. Paul was just mindin' his own business. He ought to be put away." I didn't think that talking to Jeanette would shed any new light on the fight. The girls reinforced my impression that a combination of neighborhood issues and Sandy's newness to the school was at the root of this problem.

Frannie Brooks and Mrs. Delano couldn't tell me much either. Neither had seen anything until Sandy and Paul were rolling on the ground. Mrs. Delano had tried to break them up, but they didn't appear even to hear her commands. She told me, "That Sandy is so strong! When I tried to grab hold of him, he just about tore my arm off!" The way she told it, Sandy was the aggressor and had the upper hand most of the time. Once she had failed to separate the boys, she sent Frannie for me and "just tried to keep the rest of the children away from it."

By noon, I had concluded only that Sandy was unfit to return to his classroom. I couldn't reach his mother, as she had no phone. Rodney McCarthy, our counselor/social worker, said he hadn't met her. He didn't know if she worked or not. He offered to walk over to the projects after lunch and see if he could find her. By then, Sandy was sequestered in Rodney's office, lost in the limbo of my decision making.

The facts, as I was able to reconstruct them, meant that Sandy should be suspended. He clearly had been in a fight. Whether he was the perpetrator or not, he obviously had the upper hand, so it looked as if he'd been the aggressor. Anyway, he'd used enough foul language and shown ample disrespect—behavior we've been trying to discourage—to earn him an immediate suspension. It seemed that most of the kids and many of the teachers believed that Sandy had picked the fight. For every child on the playground and most of the teachers, for justice to be done, Sandy should be thrown out of school for at least three days.

Yeah, but . . .

As persuasive as the case for suspending Sandy was, I was troubled by the sight—and the sounds—of Sandy himself. He seemed like such an underdog. He'd never gotten an even break from Jeanette and her friends. I suspect he'd wanted to play in Paul's wall-ball game as a way to get in with these kids who had been so hostile to him. When they shut him out, he became very vulnerable. Whether Paul pushed him first, or he threw the ball at Paul, Sandy's self-respect had been on the line. He really didn't have much choice but to stand up to Paul.

Everything I stand for as an educator is rooted in treating kids with respect. I really believe that until kids feel they are respected in school, they can't learn or value learning. I think that choices about discipline should take kids' social and psychological situations into account; discipline should be individualized. While it's important to have a single set of standards, how kids are handled and how punishment is meted out must be adjusted to fit each circumstance. Sandy was a newcomer to the neighborhood, at the bottom of the pecking order. Paul, Jeanette, and Starr probably reinforced this pecking order by accentuating Sandy's differentness. He had few social supports at home and had pretty much failed to break into the social order of his classroom and grade. Wasn't he a behavior problem waiting to happen?

I tried to calculate the importance of his "flipping out." Anger that makes you lose control, as if you don't care what the consequences are, is anger you cannot be personally responsible for, especially if you're eleven years old. While Sandy could have chosen not to join the wall-ball game and possibly avoid this whole fracas, could he envision at that point that it would lead to this? I tried to sort out what I would say to Sandy if and when I suspended him. How would I advise him to avoid situations like this next time?

I decided that this really wasn't all Sandy's doing. Once Paul had said, "butt out," to him, his own ego and the years of being shut out by these kids just took over. Could I hold him personally responsible for everything he did after that?

When Sandy was calmer, we talked some more, but it didn't resolve my quandary. He was still irrational about Jeanette, Paul, "and them." I was convinced that he felt deeply wounded, shut out from social contacts that mattered to him because of factors he could not control—his social group, perhaps his address, and certainly his status as a newcomer. I felt frustrated and as helpless as he was to affect these things. All I could do was treat the symptom of this societal problem. By treating the symptom according to the rules I was sworn to uphold, I felt as if I were only adding to the wrong that Sandy felt. Now I was going to align myself and the school with "the world that was screwing Sandy over."

That's when Gladys told me that central office was on the phone, and two social workers from the city were waiting for me. I thought, oh my God, three things to do at once; what the hell am I going to do with Sandy? It was what I call "cut-and-run time": if I don't dispense with Sandy within the next thirty seconds, I'll have thirty-five problems backed up at my office door. So dispense with him!

So I did. I asked myself, what are the bare facts here? Sandy had broken a serious school rule. Most students and teachers had either witnessed it or heard about it. The evidence indicated that Sandy was the perpetrator of the fight. He'd obviously been out of control. He'd disobeyed teachers, and he'd said some things he shouldn't have. This behavior clearly demanded disciplinary action, and if the disciplinary code of the school were to apply to all children, Sandy could not go unpunished.

Although I'm not proud of this, I have to admit that my own newness to the principalship may have influenced me too. I came to Southside two years ago as a young principal. All along, I've felt it important to convey to kids what is right and wrong, what they can get away with, and what they can't. This is also an important message to send to staff and parents. We need a controlled school, and I need to be an in-charge principal.

Gladys made out a five-day suspension for Sandy. I asked Rodney to take him home and tell his mother. I picked up the phone to the impatient voice of the secretary to the district superintendent for attendance.

We suspect that you have experienced a Sandy in your own work as educators, parents, and citizens. You undoubtedly recall many behavior problems, the meting out of punishment, the anguished silence of kids feeling wronged by authority. Injustices experienced as children or as adults are long-lasting and often extraordinarily painful. Memories of specific incidents, of words heard and emotions felt, and especially of the people in authority and what they said and what they did last long and vividly into adulthood. In many of these memories, the person in authority is the principal.

Gerry's internal conversation gives us a glimpse of the anguish that principals often experience in disciplinary cases. Kids bring their own issues to school every day. Many of these issues end up resting in the hands of the principal. In inner-city schools like Southside, social and cultural differences, race, and poverty will distress children. In suburban schools, clothing styles, competition for grades, or parental absence will undercut a spirit of inclusiveness. In rural schools, family histories and socioeconomic differences will divide children. When these issues create conflict with other children, with adults, or with academic and extracurricular tasks, students find themselves at odds with the formal rules and informal norms of the school.

Resolution of the student's conflict with others and with the institution itself—you see, there are two dimensions to these incidents—nearly always fall to the principal. As Gerry found, disciplinary work becomes justice work. Everyone cares deeply about resolutions because they represent how the principal and the school will care for the rights, personal safety, and integrity of each and every person at the school (Gutmann, 1987; McNeil, 1986). All too often, as Gerry found out, what seems right for the institution seems to violate what individual children need in order to grow and learn.

To tease out some of the challenges in this tension, we next share with you some key ideas from our ongoing conversation. The next sections of the chapter are letters between Richard and Gordy about Gerry's journal. We invite you to listen in and, in the final section, to engage with us in exploring some of the major issues we uncover.

Dear Gordy,

Here's how I see it: Gerry became a victim to the endless avalanche of demands on the principal and she folded. Against her better judgment, she did the expedient thing, not the right thing.

Some people will argue that she did the right thing by adhering to the rules and suspending Sandy. On the face of it, the evidence required that she throw him out: Sandy was the perpetrator; he bloodied Paul; he was disrespectful and abusive toward teachers; he used foul language; he was out of control and could have hurt others. From the standpoint of teachers, of Paul, Jeanette and "all them," and of the school as an institution requiring order, it made sense to remove Sandy. It even met the criterion of *what he deserved*. Those he'd offended felt that justice was done, and law and order were preserved.

But was justice done? Two things bother me. The first is: Gerry knew that throwing Sandy out of school had a good chance of increasing Sandy's difficulties as a person and as a student at Southside. In the "Yeah, but . . ." section of her story, Gerry was quite eloquent about the underlying factors in Sandy's life that may have led him to behave as he had. Most telling of all was her observation that Sandy probably wasn't totally in control of his own emotions and behavior. Exactly! What eleven-year-old is? It's especially hard for an eleven-year-old in Sandy's circumstances— new to the school, treated as an intruder in the neighborhood, and socioeconomically marginal—to feel he's in a predictable safe world. The fact is, he wasn't. So how could Gerry expect him to act civilized?

Gerry's a sensitive person who cares about her school's kids. She also seems like a committed educator; she wants her actions to help kids learn, grow, and become mature citizens. This is why I think she made a mistake—and knows it. Her educator side told her that an expedient suspension would not help Sandy, yet she did it anyway. In a sense, she folded to the pressure of the teachers, the dominant group of kids, and her boss's expectations that Southside be controlled. She did what the institution called for, not what Sandy's education and development called for.

I don't mean to discredit Gerry for doing this. Lord knows, I did the same thing numerous times as a principal. Rather, I mean to encourage Gerry not to become hardened to why kids act out, not to throw up her hands in these tough spots and say: what the hell, I don't have time to get to the bottom of this; I'll cut my losses and get on with school.

This raises the second reason I think Gerry was wrong. She violated her own integrity as an educator. She has to live with herself, to feel good about her decisions, if she's to maintain an optimistic and healthy view of her leadership at Southside. How many times can she compromise her judgment of what's best for individual kids and still feel good about what she's doing there? After two years as a principal, she's already learning to justify ignoring the individual needs of individual kids in order to keep the institution orderly, to satisfy some teachers' calls for consistent discipline (meted out by the principal, of course), and to establish her reputation as a strong principal.

Expediency, cutting your losses, making it through the day: call it what you will. When educators who know better start to act this way, they do injustices to themselves as well as to every child and adult. They violate a sacred trust that followers seek to place in leaders, a trust that says, When it's my turn to receive judgment, I expect you, Gerry, to respect my view of things, my needs, and my right to be here and to learn.

For Gerry's sake, I hope time has not run out for Sandy. The good news is that Gerry has tomorrow to begin building a bridge to Sandy and to devise a way that the school can respond to his needs educationally, socially, and psychologically. The suspension, if she and Rodney handle it right, is an opportunity to begin a partnership with Sandy's mother and with his fifth-grade teacher. Gerry must follow up on the fight too, so all kids and teachers can learn what their responsibilities are in it and in future incidents. She should start with Paul, Jeanette, Dawna, and Starr. Playground supervisors need to be alert to the "Sandys" and to their roles in preventing and resolving conflicts as they develop.

As time-consuming and energy-depleting as these follow-up activities are in a job that already makes tons of demands on Gerry, they are essential to creating an environment in which every person feels cared for and respected. Gerry's overriding goal as principal must not be merely to discipline kids and bring order to Southside. It must be to make every member of the Southside community know that, within the walls of the school, each person will be fairly treated according to his or her own needs.

Richard

Dear Richard,

I'm sorry, good friend, but I think you've gone too far. I agree that Gerry's got to balance these two things: keeping an orderly environment and treating each child justly, according to his or her personal and educational needs. But you take the individual side of this too far. You end up arguing for moral relativism: each child's needs must be given such a priority that the basic needs of society go out the window. I think Gerry is making Sandy's situation more complicated than it really is—and in the process making it much harder on herself.

As I reread her story and your letter, I kept wanting to say, get real! The basic facts of this situation are that Sandy attacked Paul and allowed himself to get out of control. Sure, the girls and society in general contributed to it. But won't they always? I mean, the world isn't fair. We all have to learn to live with prejudice, inequities, and challenges. Gerry shouldn't feel so bad about the fact that she can't single-handedly right all the wrongs in Sandy's life and the Southside neighborhood. First of all, that's impossible for her or the school to do. And second, if she keeps feeling bad about this situation, I think she's undercutting her own effectiveness as a principal.

She should accept the fact that one of the school's major jobs is to teach the Sandys and the Pauls the basic realities and rules of American society. Prepare them to deal with the real world. Teach them to coexist peacefully. It's unrealistic to think that they'll ever fully respect each other, let alone treat each other justly.

How should Gerry have handled this? Pretty much the way she did. She and her teachers must have clear rules and must be vigilant in their enforcement of them. They must do this in an understanding manner, as she did. But they cannot sacrifice the lesson that misbehavior has real consequences just because they see that kids aren't totally responsible for their own behavior. As you said, what eleven-year-old is? This is exactly why the adults in the school, led by Gerry, need to teach them to be responsible. Today in America, we have too many people doing what they feel like doing. Schools need to teach kids responsibility the way the real world usually does it: show them that misbehavior has negative consequences for Sandy, for those who were hurt by it, and for society in general.

This is basic to the mission of schools as social institutions: teaching young people to coexist in a heterogeneous, multicultural world by conforming to the norms of a democratic society and within the boundaries of the law. Gerry is a standard-bearer for society, as are the teachers. In this case, Gerry has a responsibility to make clear to Sandy what acceptable behavior looks like and why it's important. She needs also to show how everyone is treated equally before the law, that fair is fair. In this light, as she points out, she needs to make Paul and the girls see how their discriminating against Sandy contributes to a negative situation for all. They all have a role in this misbehavior, and they all must be made to understand how to prevent it from recurring.

If they need help with this, Gerry is fortunate to have a social worker to work with kids who are at one another's throats. If it seems useful, she should involve the parents too. But I'd caution her against overextending herself because she'll soon find herself trying to right the social wrongs of the entire community, not just the school. Frankly, that's what's burned out a lot of principals. My advice to Gerry is: work with your staff to make your school a safe, fair place for these kids, but leave the rest of the world to other people.

We'll succeed beyond our wildest dreams if we can just get the kids of today to be responsible for themselves and to respect society's rules. If they see how they're supposed to fit in, they'll understand why the justice system is such an important part of our society. Maybe they'll make the world they inherit more civic-minded and less me-first.

Regards,
Gordy

Some Leads to Pursue

You have listened in on Gerry Taylor's story and, through her eyes, have experienced a tension familiar to many principals: how can we treat every student justly when doing so may violate our institutional rules and norms? Richard and Gordy's letters highlight what is an inevitable tension between doing what is right for the majority and doing what is right for each child. We have some suggestions for thinking through this persisting—and thus never resolved—question in your own case.

We see three potentially fruitful matters to explore. First, we think principals need continually to reevaluate the school's disciplinary strategies in light of changing student and community social issues. Second, we suggest that principals should clarify the limits of their roles as justice makers. Finally, we view the principal's work with the other adults in the school's community as vital to building a *just culture* for students.

Reflecting on Gerry's story and our conversation, we are reminded that there is often widespread agreement about the goals of school discipline: to make the school a controlled and safe place, a fair place, and a place where kids can concentrate on learning, and teachers can concentrate on teaching. We establish rules, roles, and procedures to create a disciplined environment. But the real world of Gerry's school, like many schools, is far messier than the world envisioned in most of our rules and the systems of thinking that underlie them. The essence of this messiness is that our rules govern behaviors, not the conditions that generate those behaviors. When we discipline children, we treat the symptoms of social, cultural, and psychological problems. Our rules and systems do not, in and of themselves, help us to treat the problem itself unless we see each behavioral incident in its broader context. This calls for principals to consider each child and his or her own unique blend of background conditions and to ask, as Gerry asked, What is just, respectful treatment from this student's perspective?

Absent a perfect set of rules or a perfect system for making decisions about student behavior, we believe the principal is assisted by his or her capacities to judge what is fair and just in each case. To do so, principals need to be well acquainted with competing values and beliefs about student behavior and development. What do kids at different developmental levels, from different cultural backgrounds, and with varying socioeconomic positions perceive as fair? How completely can children control their behavior or anticipate consequences? Principals must stay abreast of the changing social norms of their communities and accommodate these in their thinking instead of, as Gordy's letter argued, simply imposing their own system of justice and order on all children. From this strategy, students like Sandy will simply learn that schools too can be disrespectful of who they are and where they come from. In the end, we believe, principals must accommodate each child's inherent sense of fairness to the sense of fairness that the school seeks to teach.

Ultimately, it is the principal's role to help the school make choices about students and their behavior that balance the community's interests and the child's needs. Every disciplinary decision involves this balancing act. Principals must work with children and adults alike to assure that both the school's need for order and the child's right to make mistakes and to learn from them are respected. This is very difficult work. As you pursue your own judgment making, we recommend these works: Saphier and D'Auria (1993), Strike and Soltis (1992), Kohlberg (1981), Sockett (1993), and Association for Supervision and Curriculum Development, Panel on Moral Education (1988). For a philosophical base, see Dewey (1915) and Apple (1990). Contemporary education journals, such as *Phi Delta Kappan* and *Educational Leadership*, carry timely reflections on the seemingly eternal search to sharpen our judgment about these complicated justice issues.

The second avenue we suggest is more personal: clarify your understanding of the principal's role in making the school a just place for all. Why do principals like Gerry often believe it is solely their job to legislate morality in their schools? This is clearly an impossible task. Gerry's story demonstrates so well that one person cannot have the time, the facts—as all concerned see them—the energy, or the interpersonal skills to resolve every injustice in a school. Busy principals simply cannot do it alone.

We believe schools can become just communities, but we don't see the principal as the only standard-bearer for society, as Gordy's letter suggests. Principals must be willing to let go of the belief that "if I am to care for something, I must control it" (Block, 1993). A large part of Gerry's problem is her assumption that if she could better understand Sandy and his peers, she could make things right for him and the school. Precisely what does Gerry think she can understand? Will her understanding alone teach Sandy and Paul to make reasoned judgments about what actions are desirable and how to decide to act in desirable ways? This kind of thinking leads inevitably to principals who, as they perceive themselves losing control of all the factors that shape student behavior, write more rules, send more memos, and hoard more power.

We suggest that this tendency actually leads schools and principals in the wrong direction. We have learned from the fields of psychology (Kohlberg, 1981), philosophy (Noddings, 1984), and psychotherapy (Coles, 1986) that children do not learn to be moral by learning to obey rules that others make for them (Covaleskie, 1992). Rather, they develop into morally responsible thinkers and doers by engaging in moral thought and conversation on a consistent basis, led by adults who themselves think and act in morally responsible ways. What helps children become moral is not awareness of rules alone (three strikes and you're out) but discussing the reasons for acting in moral and ethical ways.

So what does Gerry do? We suggest she adopt a role for herself as principal that frees her from being the sole or even final arbiter of justice. Justice—and discipline, in which issues of justice arise—is not only the principal's work; it is everyone's work. If you, as principal, can operate on this principle, you will not find yourself perpetually buried beneath a mound of disciplinary issues waiting for you alone to decide. You will also find that you aren't constantly forced, as Gerry was, to "cut your losses" and decide cases against your better judgment because you haven't the time to do justice to every child.

Finally, principals need to devote more energy to helping adults in the school community to think and act in a morally responsible way, so that children experience a just environment at school. Teachers are the largest part of this community, but custodians, aides, secretaries, specialists, bus drivers, and especially parents play significant roles as well. Respected educational thinkers (including Barth, 1990; Sergiovanni, 1992; Lieberman, 1988; and Noddings, 1984) tell us that the most effective and perhaps the only way to assure just treatment of all children is for all adults to act together, shaping the community around principles of justice.

To chart this course requires careful thought about how we

treat each other in school, requiring us to be sensitive to inter-personal factors in both the adult and student arenas. We suggest you consider:

- Beginning a conversation, much as we are doing, with the adults in your school about the core values, beliefs, and out-comes that should guide people's treatment of one another in the school

- Exploring, as part of this conversation, how the school might need to be restructured if the adults alone are to begin acting consistently with these values, beliefs, and envisioned outcomes

- Starting, as principal, to give authority and control to those closer to the work, like teachers, so they teach students that these core values will be the basis of judgment about actions taken in school

Our experience teaches us that children will feel that their schools are just when the adults treat each other and all children with respect, understanding, and trust (see Saphier and D'Auria, 1993; Senge and others, 1994; Block, 1993; and Carmichael, 1981).

Chapter Three

Teaching

Promoting Effective Teaching and Valuing Each Teacher

Since the early 1970s, articles, books, and workshops have increasingly advocated that principals become instructional and educational leaders (Duke, 1987). Many of these claim that principals have been overly caught up solely in the management of schools. They argue that principals, instead, should be more directly involved in setting instructional priorities and shaping the quality of teaching and learning. The assumption is that it is the principal's responsibility to shape the school's instructional program.

Easier said than done, we say! Inserting yourself into the instructional realm of your school means changing some basic norms, ones that have always been present in American schools. Teachers teach; principals manage. Teachers think: I'm the best judge of what my students need; I am the certified, trained professional in the classroom. My plate is full to overflowing with lesson plans, kids, duties, parents, and you want me to take more time for supervision and for curriculum evaluation and planning. Principals think: I should be in classrooms more, but it takes so much time and energy to observe teachers and staff and to work with them in their professional growth. How can I know what's best for the students in all cases? How can I tell what's good teaching and what isn't in all the grades and subjects in my school?

These daunting questions challenge principals every day. We believe principals must be intimately involved in the instructional life of their schools. Through that involvement, they can provide the leadership essential to the school's success as a learning center. But we know few, if any, principals who do not feel deep tensions from trying to be involved in the work of their teachers and students. The persisting question we raise in this chapter is not whether or not the principal should be involved, but *how might the principal appropriately be involved in teacher's business, which has for so long been private, specialized, and often very personal?*

Principal Carl Wesley's retrospective journal about Melissa Conroy's performance gives us a frank glimpse of one principal's struggle with this question. Carl wrote this during the late summer preceding his fourth year at Edgewood Middle School, a school of 674 students and 43 teachers. Carl's school and his staff have made major strides toward the middle school concept. But recently they have experienced a wave of questions about their effectiveness. These questions have been fueled by the excellence movement, by legislated student outcomes, and by calls for accountability. Carl feels responsible for the quality of learning at Edgewood. In this light, he has harbored questions about Melissa from the time he arrived as principal. The following journal entries resulted from a colleague suggesting that, if he truly wanted to see Melissa improve, Carl should reconstruct the history of his evaluations of her "for the record."

> From the Retrospective Journal of Carl Wesley:
>
> Teachers, parents, school board members, and even students are finding it easier and easier to question the quality of our teachers. This makes it harder and harder for me to evaluate teachers. For the past two years, I've been working intensively with Melissa Conroy, a seventeen-year veteran at this school. Since I arrived four years ago, I've had questions about how good she is. I've observed a lot of her classes, have gotten to know many of her students and some of their parents. The problem is that, as I've become increasingly certain in

my own mind that she's not a very strong teacher, I've also learned that quite a few others around here think she's doing fine.

Here is my synopsis:

Year One

When I look back, I see that I had doubts about Melissa's performance from the start. Well, maybe not from the start, but darn close. Three-and-a-half years ago, when I first visited Melissa's seventh-grade language arts classroom, my first reaction was relief. The class was orderly, the kids well behaved and busily at work. Melissa was walking the aisles, reading over shoulders, and offering quiet suggestions. Any new principal hopes to find that most teachers at least have things under control. I didn't want any hot spots that would require me to parachute in with my bag of disciplinary tricks.

It took me the whole first year to discover what was going on in Edgewood's classrooms. With everything else I was doing for the first time at Edgewood, I really couldn't get into each teacher's classroom much. Therefore, I couldn't have enough direct access to what and how they taught to form valid impressions, much less conclusions. By the end of my first year, Melissa sort of blended into my map of the whole faculty, fitting somewhere in the middle, appearing competent and solid but not a high flyer.

I suppose that's significant, in retrospect. She didn't stand out for me. I didn't see any special energy, initiative, or colorfulness. She didn't volunteer for schoolwide activities or speak up much. Perhaps subconsciously, this influenced the way I thought about her. I consider myself a career educator, and I've always set high standards for myself. I spend a lot of time at work and enjoy doing things with kids and teachers. I think I apply these same expectations to the teachers I work with. When teachers don't meet these expectations, I question their commitment, dedication, and productivity. I don't conclude that they are bad teachers, mind you; I just put them in the "not outstanding" category.

Year Two

The following fall, I observed teachers in a more structured way. I use a clinical supervision approach. I like Glatthorn's *Differentiated Supervision* (1984) philosophy but base my evaluation system on both preconferences with a teacher that build shared observation goals and postobservation conferences in which we exchange viewpoints on how it went and set goals for improvement. At that time, I asked Melissa in a preconference how she planned to engage the kids in her lesson, which was on subject-verb agreement. She seemed startled by the question. From her response, I started thinking that engagement was not a primary factor in her approach to teaching.

Over the course of the year, I observed her classes three times. Each time, I saw the same basic lesson: Melissa gave short instructional segments to the whole class, as students listened and took notes (though only about 40 percent did so). She interspersed six to eight questions to individual students throughout her twenty-minute or so presentation, then assigned exercises related to the presentation. While the students worked on these, she either walked the aisles or corrected papers at her desk (once these were homework papers handed in at the start of the period). Two of the classes involved reading short stories; the third, grammar. In the literature classes, she spent the last ten minutes on open discussion of the questions they had been working on at their seats.

I wasn't excited about these classes. Neither were the students. But try as I might in the postconferences, I couldn't put my finger on what Melissa needed to work on. I raised the issue of student engagement. Her position was that they were very engaged in listening to her and working on her assignments. I couldn't disagree. I inquired how well the kids were learning what she expected them to—thinking that some probably weren't doing too well because they were bored to tears. She said they were doing about as well as most classes—some A work, a lot of B work, and some borderline work as expected. She was proud that her grades always looked like a perfect bell curve. Her position was that the kids just come that way in these average groups. When I asked why the "low-end" kids were failing, suggesting their boredom and lack of engagement may be factors, she said something like, "I try as hard as I can with them, but they just end up quitting on me."

By the end of the year, it was clear that she was no more excited about teaching these kids than I was about her teaching. But I didn't really know what to do about it. Though Melissa wasn't teaching the way I wanted her to, she wasn't a disaster either. She was good enough. My formal evaluation at the end of the year said nothing very enthusiastic, but it wasn't very critical either. I simply didn't have enough hard data to substantiate my gut instinct. I suggested she talk to several other teachers about using cooperative learning techniques to engage kids more. I don't think she did anything though.

Year Three

Last year, my third at Edgewood, several things changed that had an effect on my approach to Melissa. First, I started a staff development committee that ran a series of workshops devoted to teaching the middle school student. My belief that the kids must be engaged – actively in learning, using all their senses through multi-modal teaching and learning activities, was reinforced. About half the faculty, not including Melissa, adopted these ideas. Many of them began working in pairs and trios, sharing ideas.

Second, the school board, in response to public criticisms of our schools, held a series of hearings on outcome-based education. Most teachers objected to these, but a small group including Melissa supported the position taken by several board members that schools needed to do a better job of holding kids accountable for their learning.

Third, the administrative team, along with a committee of teachers appointed by the teachers' association, developed a new handbook for teacher supervision and evaluation. The new evaluation criteria, though still vague, included teacher responsibility for making their teaching stimulating and engaging.

I started noticing some changes in Melissa. She was cloistering herself with a few other teachers. As some teachers informally teamed up and began using more cooperative learning strategies and other techniques, the others grew colder. They stopped having coffee with the teachers who enhanced the middle school approach and weren't as affable at staff gatherings. Melissa appeared to be a central player in this nonparticipator group, who became increasingly critical of what the more energetic and forward-thinking teachers were doing.

My observations of Melissa's teaching didn't help. I found her classrooms more traditional and duller than before. She rarely varied the lesson structure, relied heavily on seat work, insisted on grading kids strictly by "what they produce," as she put it, and made little effort to extend herself to kids having difficulty. In our conferences, I tried repeatedly to explain to her what we've learned about activity-centered teaching and how it gives all students—the highly motivated, the not-so-able, the sleepy, the rebellious—an equal chance to learn. She usually listened agreeably, nodded, but never fully concurred with my approach.

Things deteriorated when I wrote out her summative evaluation in March based on four observations between October and March. It was the first she'd received using the new evaluation system predicated on a middle school teaching philosophy. It gave me a chance to explain to Melissa that her teaching was not engaging the kids. I made three basic points, referring to them as areas of challenge for her:

1. Her failure to vary her lesson structure and teaching methods was handicapping the children who need to be stimulated through active engagement.

2. Her failure to address the needs of poorly performing students through new approaches was condemning them to little if any learning for the entire year.

3. Her reliance on seat work and homework meant that every child was, for all intents and purposes, learning on his or her own without supervision or guided practice.

The evaluation included some commendations for her classroom order and steady attention to management details.

When Melissa read the conclusions about her teaching, she went into a deep funk. I didn't see her for six days, as she withdrew into her room. I got word that she was deeply hurt. She seemed to be avoiding me. At the May faculty meeting, she sat off to the side with a few others and didn't make eye contact. I asked her to drop by the next day after school for a chat. I told her, "You don't seem to be yourself." She said she had an appointment right after school, so she couldn't.

How Things Stand Now

It's taken until now, the summer after my third year, to conclude that I have to do something about Melissa. It's eating away at me, making me dread the beginning of school. My failure with her has really affected me. And now it's bigger than just her. There's obvious resistance to my initiatives not only from her but from others in the nonparticipators group. They're only five of our faculty, but they're enough of a group to make my attempts to build a team even more difficult. Brenda, one of our middle school leaders, told me that Melissa and the other nonparticipators felt my new initiatives were destroying the school.

I feel as if I'm running a school with destructive forces in it. I mean destructive for kids too! I'm feeling very unsure about how to deal with them the way things are now.

Carl's story is all too typical in our experience, not only with beginning principals but often with veterans. He has developed an opinion about the quality of Melissa's teaching, but the demands of his job have prevented him from thoroughly documenting it or doing anything about it. Carl has contributed to the situation because he felt ill-equipped to judge Melissa's performance in a defensible manner. He avoided the inevitable conflict that would result from confronting her. Over time, he has become more convinced that Melissa is not what Edgewood teachers should be; yet, he has felt less and less able to bring her into—or put her out of—the fold.

How can principals address staff members whose performance does not match their own high expectations without creating hostility and disaffection? How do you respectfully, even supportively, critique a teacher to help him or her improve? Most principals live with this dilemma in some form: the coach who has a winning record but emotionally abuses kids every day at practice; the high school teacher who seldom gives adequate feedback to kids on their written work; the counselor who spends most of her day in her office with the door shut, talking to the same few students while others cannot get help; the janitor who does just enough to get by. We invite you to listen in as we present a couple of different approaches to Carl's situation. We suspect that you will find the seeds of your own strategy in them.

Dear Richard,

I feel as if I've been exactly where Carl is. He's trying to move the school toward improvement by taking the professional high road, but he's also inundated trying to run the school at the same time.

Carl has some great things going at Edgewood, but he's gotten them going at the expense of his supervision of teachers like Melissa.

In a way, I think he's neglected his responsibility to assure that all his teachers are as effective as they can be. With Melissa, the evidence has been mounting that she's not a strong teacher and that she won't respond to his diplomatic requests for improvement. To Carl's credit, he hasn't been ignoring this evidence. The problem is that he hasn't been paying enough attention to it, so he can't confidently conclude that she's either a good teacher or a poor teacher.

Carl needs to do *something* because the current situation is becoming more and more negative for the kids, for Melissa, and for Carl's relationship with the nonparticipators. As long as he's uncertain about her performance, Carl cannot and should not confront her with serious allegations of incompetence. Such mistakes always backfire and can cause deep distrust. Instead, Carl must take a hopeful and positive approach with Melissa. Until proven otherwise, he's got to believe that she wants to improve and that she can improve.

Carl needs to approach Melissa more honestly than he has so far. His goal is to find her developmental level, so he can address her needs appropriately (Glickman, 1992). He should devote time and energy to working with her through the fall with the goal of giving her the best opportunity to show that she wants to improve and will commit energy and time to that improvement. He should be as direct and as nonthreatening as possible. He should emphasize her right to explore ways to change and improve her teaching that are comfortable for her. Carl's support of her efforts should be unequivocal—as long as she does something to address his concerns about her performance.

This is a tough thing to pull off, requiring lots of interpersonal skills, because Carl knows Melissa is on the defensive to start with (Levine, 1989, speaks to this). He needs to extend himself to her.

I'd call her before the summer is out and invite her to talk informally about her goals for the year. He should be frank about the growing gap between them as professionals and should invite her to be honest about her feelings toward her teaching, the school and its direction, and about him and his evaluations of her performance. He should come clean that he has doubts about her performance as a teacher and add that he wants to work more closely and openly with her to resolve these doubts. Carl should express confidence in Melissa's ability to grow professionally, and he should end the conference by identifying some goals they can work on together during the fall.

Through the fall, Carl and Melissa should meet every two weeks or so to establish a professional dialogue about what teachers need to do to be successful. As much as possible, discussions should focus on specific events and on Melissa's teaching techniques. Carl should not pass judgment on these. The point is for the two of them to explore together whether these practices are beneficial for Melissa's students. Based on this, they should be able to come to some agreement about what, if anything, needs improvement. If that doesn't happen, they will at least be clear about differences in their values and their assessments of Melissa's performance.

Throughout these conversations, Carl needs to be as supportive as he can of Melissa and to encourage her to share some of her own aspirations for improving her teaching. He should offer her professional development (without necessarily compromising his own goals for her). He should strive for a level of authenticity in their relationship that allows her to express her doubts, anxieties, and even her anger at being forced into changing. While Carl is expressing his concern that she can teach more effectively, he must not write her off. He must keep a positive, noncombative attitude. In a nutshell, I am proposing that Carl give Melissa a healthy chance to show that she is willing to improve her teaching and the quality of learning for her students.

I somewhat hesitantly add a final suggestion: Carl should informally document their meetings for the purpose of being clear about their agreements concerning Melissa's performance and progress and having a record of his assistance to her. This could take the form of memos "for our eyes only" after each session. Melissa could be encouraged to include her own reflections. I am hesitant about this because documentation of this kind could drive their relationship from so-so to terrible. But up to this point, Carl has not done a good job in this arena. There's no record from Year One. There are evaluations from Year Two, but the district's evaluation criteria were vague and the summative report is positive for the most part. In Year Three, the evaluation system changed, and for the first time Melissa's performance showed up with some warts. Recently, communication between them has almost ceased, leaving a case to be made by Melissa that Carl has closed the book on her already. If done well, their memos can help both Carl and Melissa stay focused on a few central questions about her teaching and make clear their agreements—even if they're agreements to disagree. If the fall turns out to confirm Carl's doubts about Melissa, the documentation stands as an above-board record of Melissa's disinterest in improvement and/or her inability to progress.

In sum, my suggestion to Carl is to be honest in his evaluation of her work as well as in his sincerity in supporting her attempts to improve. He must appeal to her professional pride and self-respect to convince her to make an effort to improve. If she does not make that effort, Carl cannot and should not continue to abide Melissa as a member of Edgewood's faculty.

Gordy

Dear Gordy,

How many chances do you give a teacher? As I read Carl's three years with Melissa, he has well nigh closed the book on her! Why pussyfoot around with more teacher-centered conferences? Hasn't Carl given her adequate notice that she needs to improve? Hasn't she proven that she's not willing to? In fact, it seems she's gone even further by cloistering herself with like-minded colleagues and distancing herself from Carl.

My approach to Melissa would be a lot more hard-nosed and, in a way, more honest than yours. Here's how I see the situation. When Carl came to Edgewood, he didn't feel confident about his ability to judge effective teaching. On top of that, he was inundated by all the busy-ness of the principalship and being new. Unable to determine accurately whether her teaching was average or below average in the first year, he nevertheless felt she was not a very strong teacher. In Year Two, he observed Melissa and saw some things he considered undesirable in a middle school teacher (she didn't engage kids and gave them busy work). But in Year Two, Carl was using an evaluation system that didn't help him address these weaknesses with Melissa and, I think, he still lacked the confidence to approach her directly. So another year went by, and he was left with a growing sense of frustration: "She wasn't any more excited about teaching these kids than I was about her!" he wrote.

Now, at the end of Year Three, Carl sounds as though he's come into his own. Most of Edgewood Middle School's faculty are excited about the middle school concept; there's stronger consensus about how teachers should teach, and there's even a new evaluation process in place. Not only is the school moving, but the "stuck" teachers are starting to stick out (Johnson, 1990). In your letter, you seem to suggest that he back off from the evaluations he's already done. I suggest the opposite. He was specific about Melissa's performance in the March summative evaluation. I think he should now insist on a program of improvement with a very tight time frame (McGreal, 1983; Stanley and Popham, 1988). Melissa's had seventeen years to make herself the superlative professional Carl wants in his school and who we'd all want teaching our kids. She needs to get on with it or get out.

Carl should prepare a series of suggestions regarding the three areas he cited in Melissa's March evaluation, and he should set up a conference with her the second week of school. In the conference, he should refer to that evaluation and those three points and ask Melissa what goals she has set for herself to make improvements in these areas. Before the meeting is over, or perhaps at the next meeting, Carl should present his suggestions for reaching these goals and clearly indicate his plan to conference-observe-conference with her monthly, focusing on these goals and any other issues that arise. These meetings should be followed by a written summary of the plan to be signed by both Carl and Melissa.

I think Carl's hardest task will be to confront Melissa with this plan and then to follow through on it during the year. He sounds intellectually certain about Melissa's weaknesses as a teacher, but he doesn't sound so interpersonally or politically confident. I would be sure to speak with the superintendent or personnel director to be certain that central office was prepared to support a confrontation over performance (many are not!). I would also seek among my friends or professional associates some advice on handling the feelings that will arise. Melissa is likely to fight this strategy and might very well include her support group and the teachers' association and maybe even supporters in the community. Conflict, anger, hostility, and personal/professional verbal assault could be directed at Carl. He should prepare his own support system to help him get through this without completely depleting his emotional energies.

I recommend this approach because I think it's more expeditious and more honest than the one you suggest in your letter. Carl seems convinced that Melissa's performance is hampering kids' learning and starting to divide the faculty. He needs to make this very clear to her and give her an honest chance to engage in improvement. He cannot go on, as you suggest, hoping that Melissa sees the light and writes a professional improvement plan for herself. Carl needs to get his act together—and have her get her act together by next spring. If she doesn't, he will have two-plus years of documentation of weak teaching and should move to dismissal.

Richard

Some Paths Through the Thicket

Studies of principals and the principalship have consistently shown that the tide of administrative events in schools engulfs even well-intentioned principals like Carl, leaving them few opportunities for instructional supervision, evaluation, and leadership (McGreal, 1983). Carl's story and Gordy's and Richard's letters reveal just how complex this challenge can be, drawing not only on principals' technical knowledge but also on their interpersonal skills and personal courage. We next explore some approaches to the question raised in this chapter: how can principals address issues of performance with staff members while also supporting and respecting them personally?

One thing seems clear to us: the principal must first commit to the goal of instructional effectiveness for every teacher. Carl believes that good teaching is important, and he wants Melissa to be a good teacher. He believes he has an obligation to be involved in teachers' business and to help Melissa be a good teacher. Research on principals demonstrates that this type of significant commitment makes a real difference to the quality of instruction in a school (Smith and Andrews, 1989).

Beyond making this philosophical commitment, however, the principal will face a host of how-to questions: what does it mean for Carl to help Melissa be a better teacher? Does Melissa even want help? What exactly is the nature of a helping relationship? Gordy's letter advocates helping Melissa in a direct yet nonthreatening way. Carl should help her explore and feel comfortable about change. His support should be unequivocal—as long as she addresses his concerns about her performance. Richard's letter suggests a more hard-nosed approach, asserting that Melissa must improve her teaching . . . or else, that she needs to get on with it or get out.

These two positions seem quite different at first. Gordy's approach stresses collaboration and the importance of both parties investing and trusting in the process. Carl needs to salvage his supervisory relationship with Melissa. He must provide the opportunity for both of them to come to terms with his concerns about her performance. Richard's letter emphasizes Melissa's responsibility to maximize her teaching effectiveness. Melissa seems to have neglected her professional obligation by ignoring Carl's three-year effort to discuss her effectiveness. Richard's letter takes the position that Melissa has rejected Carl's help. She must now sink or swim on her own.

In another light, these two approaches are really not so far apart. Gordy and Richard both accept Carl's premise that helping Melissa to change means *change or else*. They all believe a principal can legitimately decide how and if a teacher will perform her teaching duties. This is the essence of evaluation versus supervision. Central to supervision is the sharing of professional improvement between supervisor and supervisee; it assumes equality in their roles and collaboration in their efforts (Saphier, 1993; Glickman, 1992). Evaluation usually means one person makes judgments about the work of another. This creates an unequal relationship. Teachers often lose autonomy and feel less safe than they do either on their own or in a supervisory relationship (Stanley and Popham, 1988; Duke, 1987).

In both cases the principal is making decisions about the teacher based on observations. Although Gordy suggests that Melissa be given a chance to join in this decision-making authority, it's on Carl's terms, not Melissa's. Richard states that Carl should address Melissa's apparent mediocrity by drawing a line in the sand immediately. In both cases, Melissa has less authority and autonomy because Carl assumes he must assert control over her work.

The crux of the issue is: can a principal truly help a teacher improve by lessening the teacher's authority and autonomy? When you know that a teacher is doing a mediocre or poor job, is it justifiable to exercise such power?

We suggest that principals and prospective principals explore these questions as they develop habits of supervision and evaluation that will help teachers serve their students most effectively. We offer four observations to assist you in this exploration:

First, it is helpful to examine your knowledge of effective teaching, so you are confident that you know what makes some teaching more effective. Can Carl be confident that his judgment of Melissa's performance is right? She is not teaching the way he would teach, but is it the right way for her? We suggest that to improve teaching quality, principals must be knowledgeable about teaching, how its effectiveness is established, and how it can be improved.

This knowledge is technical in nature. We are fortunate to have a growing body of literature about teaching (Saphier and Gower, 1987). The literature on supervision is also very helpful in the crucial arena of establishing valid observations of significant teaching and learning events (Glickman, 1992; Acheson and Gall, 1980). Without a grounding in the core technical knowledge, principals might find it difficult to engage with teachers in open informed conversation about their effectiveness.

Second, this knowledge does neither Carl nor Melissa any good nor can they use the knowledge unless their relationship is one of equal respect. This relationship hinges on each one's assumptions about the other. Is Melissa resting on her reputation? Is she resisting Carl because she doesn't want to change? Because she resents his authority? Because she knows no way to change? From Melissa's viewpoint, is Carl coming after her? Is it right for him to insist that all the teachers conform to this new middle school stuff? How can he require her to change when he's never taught English? Melissa's reading of Carl's motives and of his faith in her will set off emotions in her that will color their interactions and powerfully sculpt their relationship. The same holds for Carl's reading of Melissa.

Deeply important interpersonal capacities come into play on the part of the principal. We suggest that you use Carl's case to explore these capacities in yourself. To build the type of strong relationship that will help a teacher improve requires the principal to be open and authentic. This means being willing to listen and to understand as well as being able to express ideas and feelings trustfully. These processes are taken up in Glickman's (1985) basic text, *Supervision of Instruction: A Developmental Approach,* and in Levine's (1989) very helpful book, *Promoting Adult Growth in Schools: The Promise of Professional Development.* Argyris and Schön (1974) provide an excellent framework for understanding interpersonal action, and Senge (1990b) sets forth some conditions in which authentic communication can occur.

Our third observation deals with Carl's difficult choice: to bring the issue of Melissa's performance to a head or not. Is it worth tearing the faculty apart and perhaps ending Melissa's teaching career to get the improvement he wants? Clearly, Melissa has fallen short of Carl's standard for effective professional performance. Does holding to his standards justify souring relationships on the faculty— between Carl and the nonparticipators, between middle school advocates and nonparticipators, and even between teachers' association stalwarts and others? What makes Carl so certain about his standards anyway?

This quandary has ethical and political dimensions for the principal. Once you have decided that it is largely your responsibility to monitor the quality of teacher performance, you may find yourself feeling solely responsible for the fallout. The result can be a principal running at top speed to patch up relationships, shore up morale, and make the evaluation case hold up—all at the same time. In our experience, this rapidly degenerates into a *lose-lose* scenario that will balkanize the faculty and burn out the principal (Donaldson, 1991). Clearly, another approach is called for.

And this leads to our fourth observation. Carl and Melissa operate within a larger system of people—faculty, staff, students, parents, central office, school board, community—all of whom have an interest in Melissa's teaching performance and Carl's competence as an evaluator and leader. Carl and Melissa both need to recognize that when anyone raises questions about the quality of learning in the school, the repercussions touch everyone. This perspective acknowledges interdependence between Carl and Melissa and their mutual obligation to strengthen the school community's work with children, not to impair it.

From this perspective, Melissa is a responsible person with ongoing obligations to control and improve her own performance and her contributions to the school. She must have regular opportunities to exercise these obligations. She deserves valid feedback on her work, time to reflect on its meaning, and chances to develop new knowledge and skills. Most important, she needs to feel support and respect; she needs to feel trusted to make free and informed choices as she explores alternatives for her own growth as a teacher (Blase and Kirby, 1992).

Carl is also part of a professional community that needs to assist not just Melissa but all teachers, parents, and principals to become more effective in their work with children. We suggest you think further about the principal's role in this community. In particular, we invite you to question what it means to lead in such a community. Is Carl ultimately responsible for all these people? We think not. Is he then first among equals? Again, we think not (Wheatley, 1992, and Senge, 1990a, would agree). We see the principal's role as helping the school community to articulate its standards—not the principal's standards—and facilitating better ways to fulfill these standards for everyone.

The principal's leadership in this timeless endeavor is extraordinarily important. It involves developing a culture of learning and teaching in which the examination of practice is an everyday activity, one supported by collegial relationships, time, and appropriate technical skills (Little and McLaughlin, 1993; Lieberman, 1988; Blase and Kirby, 1992). Change cannot be the overriding value, as it seemed to be in Carl's case. Serving children's learning and developmental needs must be. The culture of professional reflection must generate valid information about what adults do and how it affects the growth of students. Improving relationships through practice-centered dialogue among all adults, not just between the Carls and the Melissas, is the only practical vehicle for determining what change in practice is needed.

We leave you with this suggestion: principals need most to spread the responsibility and the resources for optimal performance among everyone. Hoarding or controlling them simply does not work for the school or for the principal. Think of how ineffective the current system of teacher evaluation and school accountability is in most places. We challenge you to take our observations and pursue them in discussions with colleagues, reading the resources, and in your own practice. This is our attempt to spread the responsibility and the resources for our effectiveness as a profession to you.

Chapter Four

Purpose

Integrating Process and Product

Since the time of Thomas Jefferson, schools have been called upon to foster the educational achievement and the social development of students. These fundamental purposes continue to influence what is taught, what is emphasized, and what parents and community expect from schools. These goals are pursued in a variety of ways, often creating conflict and generating disagreement among teachers, parents, and citizens. Both the conflicts and the divergent expectations are the bailiwick of the principal.

Educational achievements have traditionally been linked to measurable outcomes in academic disciplines and in extracurricular activities such as athletics and the arts. By and large, educational successes have been determined by what is measurable and quantifiable, such as students' attainment of further educational or employment goals. Underlying assumptions have been that learning is ultimately an independent achievement and that competition is good for learning, leading to higher standards and excellence. This view emphasizes the "ends" of education. Advocates focus on measurable results and specified outcomes, not on how one reaches them.

Other less visible school purposes coexist with the dominant measurable achievement approach. John Goodlad, in his epic study of American schools (1984), found that most parents care deeply about schools' influence on children's personal and social development. Many parents believe that schools should foster cooperation, civic responsibility, self-discipline, respect for authority, and other positive characteristics. Historically, these qualities have been the domain of

51

student management. Recently they have become central to curriculum initiatives. In high schools, for example, social, personal, and civic development are the goals of community-service projects and integrated curriculum. Middle and elementary schools have reorganized their structures to provide interdisciplinary and cooperative learning activities that are child-centered and developmentally appropriate. Advocates of these curricula focus on what children learn from the activities, culture, and process of schooling, believing that the "means" of education are the "ends" that schools should emphasize.

How do schools both produce learned scholars with proven records of achievement and also nurture in children the processes that will make them self-confident and well rounded? How do school leaders mediate the conflicts generated by differing views on these goals among members of the school community? Principals face this tension every day. Is it contradictory to root for the basketball team to beat its rival and at the same time encourage children in the elementary grades to help one another learn? Should we recognize academic and athletic prowess in some when we know it deflates the self-confidence of others?

This chapter's story comes from Sue Ann Podolski's third year as principal of Fort Morrison Elementary School, a grade–two-through-six school in a fast-growing suburb in the Southwest. From it we explore the tension of balancing product and process.

Thursday Afternoon's Faculty Meeting

On a spring Thursday afternoon, Sue Ann sits with the thirty-seven other professional staff members in a classroom that has been hastily reorganized for a faculty meeting. During a lull late in the meeting, grade-five and -six teachers Ted, Paula, and Manny have once again raised concerns about the language arts preparation their kids are getting in the earlier grades. Shari and Foster have leapt to the defense of their second- and third-grade colleagues' curriculum. Let's listen in.

Ted: We're hearing it from all sides that our kids don't have the basic reading and writing skills for junior high and, you know, I agree. Seriously, Sue Ann, we can't put off looking at our language arts curriculum any longer.

Paula: Ted's right. We've been roasted one too many times on the state assessment tests. We've got a different group of parents in town than we did nine years ago when we went to whole language and learning centers. They want their kids coming out of Fort Morrison with good basic skills, so they can excel at middle school.

Sue Ann: Paula, I wonder if we could save this until . . .

Shari: No, Sue Ann, we can't put this off any longer. Ted and Paula are right, and it sounds to me as though we're not all supporting what we're doing in the lower grades anymore. We gotta clear the air on this one.

Foster: I agree. Frankly, I'm tired of it too. I mean are we going to stand together for our language arts program or backslide? You know, Ted, we've put an incredible amount of time in on this to get it where it is. The program is successful at getting kids to feel comfortable with writing and reading. And our portfolios show that nearly every child does perform eventually at grade level.

Manny: But Foster, you can't keep sticking your head in the sand. The world out there doesn't cut kids slack if their learning style is different. Hey, we're not helping these kids a bit by just making them feel good.

Shari: Hold on there. Our job isn't just to turn out little spellers and punctuators. I think we're being swayed too much by the back-to-basics people, those business people who sat on the blue ribbon panel and decided what's wrong with the schools. As if they knew. They're just looking for little automatons they can hire at minimum wage!

Sue Ann: That's a little harsh, Shari. Let's keep this on a civil plane, okay? We have four minutes left in the meeting. How many of you think we should take this up at next week's meeting? *Twenty-three hands go up, including nearly every fifth- and sixth-grade teacher's.*

Ted: We've been talking about this at our grade level meetings for a long time. We want to look at grading and retention policies too. We've been passing kids along, waiting for the quote developmentally appropriate unquote moment to teach them what they need. We . . .

Sue Ann: Thank you Ted. We are aware of that point of view. Most of us want to take it up next week. Let's adjourn and I'll get you an agenda for next week's meeting by Monday.

The faculty bursts out in hushed conversations. Most huddle in two large groups: upper-grade teachers around Ted, Paula and Manny; lower-grade teachers around Shari and Foster. Sue Ann busies herself with her notes and is relieved when Jamal approaches her with a question about an entirely different topic.

Later that afternoon, Sue Ann sits in her office sipping a Diet Pepsi, mulling over the meeting and her options. Her thoughts whirling from one thing to another, she thinks about whether or not to encourage a debate that seems ready to break out into civil war:

> Shari's right. This all goes back to that blue ribbon panel from last spring. Those two new board members were elected pushing that line about holding us more accountable for learning outcomes. I mean, these people are pretty shortsighted—they believe the country's going backwards, and we've lost our competitive edge economically and every other way because we don't keep kids' noses close enough to the grindstone. These are the same people who

think we've let schools get out of control and it's messing up society, instead of the other way around.

Why is it that educators are the only ones who see it as it really is? These kids are dealt to us with so many needs they can't learn the three R's by the old rote method. The developmentally appropriate route works so much better because kids discover that learning is a natural, productive, and enjoyable activity. As our motto says: they learn to be learners and that lasts for a lifetime. The problem is that all the wonderful things they learn and the skills and affective benefits don't show up on the standardized tests. I mean, we know the outcomes are there, and more kids are learning, but we keep getting hammered by the public and the junior high teachers because they're looking for something else.

What to do? Well, we're committed to talking about it next week, and my job will be to referee, I guess. Perhaps we'll start by having each side highlight the pros and cons of its position. I'll ask Crystal to keep notes on chart paper, so we can keep it all public. Maybe we can take a look at this more objectively.

The Next Thursday and Afterward

Sue Ann follows through with her idea of making public the various viewpoints on tightening up the language arts curriculum. The meeting is spirited but civil, and many points of view are expressed. After an emotional hour, Sue Ann has sheets of chart paper plastered to the bookcases and chalkboard. She asks Ted, Paula, Shari, and Foster to join her in forming a subcommittee to sort out the major arguments and bring them back to the faculty for decision making.

The subcommittee meets three times over the next two weeks. The meetings grow heated at times as Shari and Ted, especially, try to convince each other of their positions. Tensions grow over the following two weeks. The faculty's private conversations simmer over curriculum disagreement and growing personal criticism from other staff. Worried that the division in her faculty might become irreparable, Sue Ann urges the four to come to an agreement on what they see as the issues. They produce a document for faculty deliberation. Here's the beginning of it:

March 17
To: Fort Morrison Faculty
From: Ted, Paula, Shari, Foster, and Sue Ann

We've finally put together our summary of the February 27 meeting. Please look it over and come to Thursday's meeting with your views and suggestions on the direction Fort Morrison should be taking. Thanks for your help and patience.

Question One: what should we be teaching in language arts?

Points of view expressed:

- Lifetime skills: teach literature-based and writing-based curriculum that invites students to use all kinds of communication—speech, writing, reading, electronic, keyboarding, and so on.
- Specific skills needed for the next grade: go back to the scope-and-sequence chart and teach specific skills in an orderly way. We can't work on all literacy skills at the same time. Make sure nobody moves on until they get what they're supposed to get at each grade.
- Appreciation of literature and human expression: language arts are tools for communicating experience. We must help kids learn to use them for their own purposes. Integrate the arts, music, and other forms of expression with writing and reading. Make them relevant to kids' experiences.
- Some combination of these.

Question Two: how will we demonstrate to parents and the public that students are getting what they need?

Points of view expressed:

- Administer standardized tests. Use gradewide tests four times a year to measure progress, and link promotion to these. Go back to the old rank card with numerical grades. Kids learn best when they're challenged to meet a standard. The real world is like this. We can get remedial help faster to the kids who fail.
- Use portfolios that demonstrate each student's progress in all areas of language arts—self-expression, grammar, logical thinking, creativity, neatness, and so forth. Keep developmental notes on each child in these areas. Enlist parents to reinforce activities at home. Kids have different maturity levels and learning styles. Forcing them to meet standards they aren't ready for turns them off to learning and school. Language arts are about communication and thinking skills, not just grammar and mechanics.
- Some combination of these.

Question Three: should we increase our language arts time?

Points of view expressed:

- No. We spend too much time on them now and don't have enough science and social studies. We just need to teach them more efficiently.
- No. Language arts are used all the time, all day long. We should be integrating them by teaching them in all subjects and activities.
- Yes. The problem seems to be in grades five and six. So expand the language arts block, but don't go to homogeneous grouping.
- Yes. We all need to pay more attention to how each child is doing. We need more time to keep track of this. Maybe hire a language arts coordinator.

Sue Ann, it seems, is being propelled forward by a wave of concern that has its origins in the ocean of interests, hopes, and expectations of parents, citizens, teachers, and even students. In the recent past, the school has changed its language arts teaching to adapt to "where each child is." Classroom activities have diversified so that each child's experience shapes itself to his or her capabilities and learning style. While it appears to the teachers that many students are flourishing in this setting, it has become more difficult to demonstrate to parents and the public that each child has attained a minimum competency in language arts skills. It is as if one tide—the learning *process* is most important—has started receding and another tide—the learning *product* is most important —has begun coming in.

Sue Ann's challenge is many-sided. She must again face just what the basic purposes of Fort Morrison are. Linked to this is the more difficult task of fashioning teaching and learning strategies that do justice to both process and product. Perhaps more challenging, however, are the growing divisions within the faculty over the philosophical debate. Her faculty seems to be on the brink of blaming one another for their collective deficiencies. They have fallen into an either-or mind-set: it's either our way or no way. Your way is impossible to support.

Sue Ann is confronted with multiple and seemingly competing standards. All points of view are offered genuinely in the service of what each person believes is the way to develop a well-educated person. Sue Ann wonders if it is reasonable, possible, or even desirable to reach common agreement around an issue that reflects such deep underlying differences. She must also reconcile where she stands on the issue. What should be taught in language arts? Finally, assuming it is important to come to consensus on the issue, what is the best way to achieve it?

To begin to shed some light on Sue Ann's predicament, let's look at letters Richard and Becky recently wrote to each other about this tension.

Dear Becky,

Sue Ann should have seen this conversation coming her way during her first year at Fort Morrison when Manny asked the group
somewhat sarcastically at a faculty meeting, "When *exactly* is it
important for our kids to know the capital of Florida?" Someone
responded, "When they figure out that Florida is a state and not a
country!" There was nervous laughter in the room, but the staff
never really entered into the discussion seriously. She should have
known she was in it then.

On first glance, two questions come up: what standards are
important to Fort Morrison, and to whom are they important? Sue
Ann is probably painfully aware there is no shortage of "whoms"
around the school. They include teachers, parents, the Fort Morrison community, the school board, and of course, the students.
She's more than likely also aware that purposes and standards are
by no means the unique concern of Fort Morrison.

She's old enough to remember the concern that *Sputnik* pro-
duced and later the consternation that followed the release of *A
Nation at Risk* (National Commission on Excellence in Education,
1983). Today, our federal and state governments as well as the
media constantly remind us that we are in not only an arms race
but also an education race. And a race, by definition, is competi-
tive. So in a peculiar way, whether Sue Ann likes it or not, the
question she faces as a principal is not only what is important in
the Fort Morrison community but what is important in schools in
general? By what authority does Sue Ann, a principal, presume to
know what is the best way for language arts to be taught?

My advice to Sue Ann is to come down as a pragmatist on this
question, as a realist and not an apologist. A school is as good as its
teachers, and Fort Morrison is as good as the teachers that currently work there. For me, the center of change is the teacher; the
central location is the classroom and the school. Language arts are
typically, and perhaps narrowly, thought of as reading and writing.

That is how most teachers think about them. Ted, Paula, and Manny are not willing to view language arts in a different way. It's not the way they were taught and not the way they prefer to teach.

Realistically, Sue Ann cannot make these teachers willing and able to foster organic individualized methods. If there were teachers at Fort Morrison willing and able to do this, Sue Ann could afford to agree with Foster, Shari, and the others who argue that the journey is the reward and have genuinely put some of their money where their mouths are. They truly have helped their kids to feel comfortable with writing and reading and have worked very hard to develop a system of assessment that reflects students' individual progress. But it appears that Foster and Shari are rare and a minority at Fort Morrison who have tried without success to interest and even teach their colleagues about whole language. So Sue Ann has to focus on accountability.

Second, Sue Ann shouldn't be an apologist for what is or is not going on at Fort Morrison. Even if there were a core group of teachers willing and able to embrace a view of language arts that is greater than the literal use of language or the ability to write precise standard English, how could we know that every student is having a rich literary experience? How could we describe it? Louis Armstrong says, "If they don't know, how are you gonna tell them?" This is the position Sue Ann would be in. Educators are responsible for evaluating the result of their work and reporting what students are learning or not learning. In fact, the same discussion should be going on with the seventh- and eighth-grade teachers that is currently taking place with the second- and third-grade teachers.

Richard

Dear Richard,

Wow! Sue Ann has her hands full with a faculty that's been drawn into a totally unproductive argument for which there is no answer, that is: product versus process. Maybe my age is showing, but when debates have continued for years and even decades, I don't think it's wise to counsel Sue Ann to take sides. Instead, I think it's time to take a look at the way the question is being framed. In my mind, this is particularly true in the debate around product and process. People are so quick to take a side in this debate, but I think it's a false dichotomy.

I have yet to see a product that didn't involve a process, and it would be difficult to go through a process if one weren't headed for a product. It clearly isn't a question of either-or. It's a whole series of complex questions including: how process is integrated with product, what teachers focus on as important, and how we evaluate and communicate what we are doing.

In any event, Sue Ann has some work to do with her staff on two counts. The first is to address how they communicate with one another. I suspect this is a result of how they relate to one another in general. Resolving that is a long-term project. But Sue Ann can take some short-term steps to improve the communication. Her second task is to help them see how complex this issue is and to avoid this simplistic either-or thinking. It can be a wonderful growth opportunity for everyone if she can move them to a higher plane.

At the risk of sounding controlling, Richard, Sue Ann needs to lay some ground rules for the next meeting. I suggest she send a letter to her staff that goes something like this:

Dear Colleagues,

I've been thinking about our last meeting. I'm concerned about the way we are communicating with one another. It's such a difficult task to meet the needs of all the children at Fort Morrison. We can't afford to drain our energies in struggles with one another. Life's too short!

I don't expect us to agree on everything. In fact, disagreement is healthy. There is nothing more energizing than a good philosophical debate. We can all learn by listening to different perspectives. I am asking that this disagreement be placed in the following context:

We're in this together. The success of Fort Morrison is contingent on how well we work together and sort out difficult issues pertaining to what children need to know and how we provide them with it. Let's view this process as an opportunity to model critical thinking and dialogue for our students. Please consider the following points:

- We're discussing a complex issue. Viewing issues as sides rather than as differing perspectives is not useful to the conversation.
- Generalities are not useful to the conversation; statements should be defended.
- Personal attacks and criticisms are not productive in the conversation.
- Time must be taken to define terms. This is true of: whole language, language arts program, accountability, and developmental education.
- No quick decisions are about to be made concerning the language arts program. It will be more of an evolution— a process of looking at what's best for children—than a revolution.
- Though topics such as retention are pertinent, we need to take one issue at a time. Now we're dealing with the language arts curriculum.

Sue Ann's role is to help the faculty become more knowledgeable about the topic before the next meeting. They are bringing many simplistic mind sets to the conversation. They seem to believe that the whole language approach and the teaching of basic writing and reading skills are in opposition. They're polarizing the other's position as: making the students feel good versus turning out little spellers and punctuators. How quickly we accept what we hear in the media when we should know better.

There are some assumptions being made about what is going on in classrooms. That suggests that Sue Ann should provide substitutes and arrange for the faculty members involved to visit one another's classrooms. I am sure they will be surprised at what they see. My bet is there will be the teaching of phonics and basic skills in what they're calling whole language classrooms and the teaching of spelling and punctuation within some very rich literary lessons in the fifth- and sixth-grade classrooms. I suggest disseminating a few well-chosen articles on developmental education and the integration of whole language and phonics.

My experience also suggests that the faculty may need to be reminded where to find the latest documents that represent the language arts curriculum. Probably there are teachers who can't locate theirs, and others who live religiously by them. Everyone should come to the meeting knowing that the curriculum does exist and the various ways it is used.

I would suggest that Sue Ann facilitate the next meeting by backing up a bit and beginning a series of meetings with the staff, brainstorming the answers to three questions bigger and more productive than process versus product. The first: what do we want students to know in language arts by the time they leave Fort Morrison at the end of the sixth grade? The second: by what indicators can we determine they do know? The third: what do we need to do to make this happen?

This should lead to rich discussions, and my bet is there would be quite a bit of agreement among the staff. A core of basic knowledge would be part of it, but I am certain that thinking skills, research skills, and attitudes would emerge also. Then the great debate begins. How do we teach students what we want them to know? This involves teaching strategies, areas of emphasis, and accountability.

I believe strongly that once you have agreement on the what, the how should be left to the teacher. Some teachers may choose to use what they call the whole language approach; others may not. Sue Ann's role could be to clarify definitions and strategies and to keep lines of communication open, that is—be a process person, Sue Ann.

You probably can tell that you've pushed a few of my buttons. I could go on forever on this topic. It's a big problem in schools that we so often don't set aside time to take a close look at these questions. Newspapers and magazines are guilty of reporting the issue simplistically as a debate between process and product. That's forgivable. They don't know any better. Why are we educators guilty of failing to get to the essence of what we're all about, of deciding what children need to know, and how they learn best? We know better.

Frustrated,
Becky

Balancing the Need for Easy Answers with the Reality of Complex Solutions

The tension around process and product permeates schools. It's difficult to explore curriculum without asking what are the roles of process and product and how do they interact. Likewise, it is impossible to reflect on leadership without exploring the staff process and how it relates to the end product. This is brought home in the question, does the end justify the means? It is our contention that school leaders today must be astutely aware of the interaction between the two and how one affects the other.

Unfortunately, the story at Fort Morrison is all too familiar to each of us. We've all been embroiled in conversations that are cyclical in nature with no resolution. More often than not they break down into an either-or debate looking for the simplistic right answer. We believe this is due to two very strong forces.

The first is the public's demand for easy answers. More than ever the public is calling for accountability in the form of good test scores, good grades, and quick precise decision making. The public's desire for simplistic answers stems from the fact that everyone's perspective on schools is very personal and emotionally charged. Parents see it from the perspective of their child's individual needs. Business people see it from their need for skilled employees. Politicians see it from their need to deliver to the public. Because everyone has had a personal involvement in school, each comes to the issue with some expertise, expectations, and investment.

The second and countervailing force is that there are no simple right answers in schools. Those who are intimately engaged in education realize that any discussion must be brought into the context of a specific school. Richard highlights this in his letter when he suggests that Sue Ann's response must be considered within the framework of an assessment of her teachers' skills. All three of us have watched a teaching strategy or curriculum unit work well one year only to be a disaster the next. We have been reminded repeatedly through the years that most decisions in education need constantly to be revisited, each year taking into account all of the factors that surround each decision: the individual makeup of the children, the strengths and interests of the teaching staff, the dynamics among the staff, the overall direction of the school, the pressures within the community. It is the process of searching for these unique answers for each context that keeps us involved in the eternal balancing.

Where do we see the principal in the balancing of this tension? We believe it is the principal's role to assist parents, school board members, and the community to understand the complexities within the school. The principal needs to alert them to the weakness of simplistic answers. The principal must also encourage the staff not to move too hastily into decisions without considering all the factors and implications of those decisions. With respect to curriculum issues, the principal should resist the impulse to respond with quick answers. Instead, the leader's job is to create an environment in which staff are engaged in the ongoing questioning of practice and are comfortable dealing with the ambiguity of having no universally correct answers from year to year. In other words, the principal must bring everyone into the process of making sense.

Dewey presents a strong case in *Experience in Education* against viewing educational theories as either-or. His aim was to bring about a discussion of some questions that were unproductively dividing American education into camps early in the century. Dewey states, "It is the business of an intelligent theory of education to ascertain the causes for the conflicts that exist and then, instead of taking one side or the other, to indicate a plan of operations proceeding from a level deeper and more inclusive than is represented by the practices and ideas of the contending parties" (p. v).

Thus, the staff become engaged in creating their own educational theory within its unique context. The principal as instructional leader nurtures an environment that encourages the construction of such theories—a climate that invites risk taking, forums for critical dialogue, and encourages a comfort level for dealing with ambiguities. The principal helps staff to develop the necessary skills for engaging in theory making themselves. Of course, this is as difficult as trying to produce the simple right answers for the public, but we contend that it's far more fruitful for students, teachers, and the school as a whole.

There are no easy steps to follow in the process of creating such an environment. We have found the journey to be one of the most exciting parts of our principalships. Each of us has used very different techniques to keep the dialogue going and would like to share a few suggestions.

Modeling

What we've found useful for leaders to keep in mind is how they might model the product that everyone is trying to achieve throughout the process of working with staff. For example, the quest for students to develop thinking skills must engage staff in the process of developing their own thinking skills. Likewise, the goal of shared decision making cannot be mandated.

In Emerson's words, "What you are . . . thunders so that I cannot hear what you say" ("Social Aims," 1876). Probably the most powerful tool a school leader has is that of modeling. We have found, however, that it requires a constant internal struggle, examining whether or not we're behaving according to our beliefs. We constantly play this thought in our heads: if I believe in thus and such, then I must do thus and such. In regard to the tension discussed here, the thought becomes: if I believe in an environment in which critical dialogue is of great importance, how might I model it?

Here are some of our answers:

- Listen closely to everyone; share my thinking and my beliefs with staff, and explain how those beliefs have been changed by hearing others.
- Exhibit my own tolerance for ambiguity by avoiding a rush to closure with simple solutions that might result in breaking down to an either-or situation. Be willing to defend this concept to the public.
- Honor differences among staff, and make it known how each contributes to the whole.
- Learn constantly and add to the dialogue through my own reading, writing, attending courses, workshops, and so forth. Engage in any staff development that is offered.
- Acknowledge that I make mistakes, and reveal them to others, including how I learn from them.
- Make forums for such dialogue a priority. I may have to give up faculty time, provide release time for teachers, or substitute myself at times for teachers so that they can work with one another. Above all, do not overload teachers with so many new projects that there isn't time to have a thoughtful dialogue.

Awareness of Vocabulary

In an effort to help staff refrain from breaking down into either-or arguments and to keep the dialogue going, be aware of the importance of language. As we have monitored ourselves over the years, we have found it helpful to purge certain words from our vocabularies. As we have gained greater awareness of our use of the language, we have realized how much we fueled the notion of either-or thinking in the past. For instance, we no longer ask different *sides* to present. Instead we ask people to listen to various *perspectives*. We refrain from making references to battling or debating, instead choosing the words discuss, learn from one another, stretch our thinking.

Another distinction we find important is the use of the word *grow* in relation to staff and school rather than the word *change*. If we truly believe that schools evolve as staff construct their own theories, then aren't we talking about more of an evolutionary growth process than a distinct change? Doesn't this approach express less judgment and more faith in staff growth than does a preconceived notion as to how they should change?

As we have grown in this area, we have become clearer in our commitment to keeping people engaged in a dialogue. Changing our vocabulary has enhanced the dialogue as well as our own beliefs. Perhaps they're interactive. Developing an awareness of how we present things to others has been a valuable growth experience for us.

Providing the Appropriate Forums and Food for Thought

Becky expressed frustration in her letter about not getting to the essence of what educators are all about. We've each experienced this frustration even when we consciously have tried to avoid it. We entered the principalship committed to being educators and not getting bogged down with managing. We vowed that our faculty meetings would be a critical dialogue about what is best for children and how the school would provide it. We envisioned our-selves as facilitators of energizing, philosophical debates—the kind that would pull us all into education. Our faculty meetings would cover only meaningful issues. We would provide seminars, panel discussions, and fireside chats for parents, administrators, and teachers together. We would engage the community in discussions about education.

We still believe this is the highest priority but humbly recog-nize what a struggle it can be to make it so. As Covey proposes in *First Things First* (1994), engage in that which is important, and the crises that have pulled you away from engaging in such things may diminish.

An effective way to convey the message that ongoing critical dialogue is honored is to share research, articles, and one's own writ-ing on the topic. It is important that people receive a variety of per-spectives and that literature on the topic continue to flow even when staff members think a decision has been made. Keep the dia-logue going. Feed it.

Asking the Bigger Questions

When we see staff members, parents, school board members, or the community engaged in futile either-or debate, we have found it use-ful to step back and ask, what are the real questions here? For exam-ple, many districts are engaged in the debate around standardized testing and alternative assessment. The question often boils down to which method of assessment is better. Framing the issue this way usually polarizes people. In our experience, we've found that explor-ing a series of questions is more productive. What is it we want to assess? What is the purpose of assessment? Who is the audience? What form of assessment most effectively informs each audience of what students know? How do each of these forms of assessment inform the learning process for students?

We find that rather than engaging in a discussion of standardized tests versus alternative assessment, it is more useful to acknowledge the many forms of assessment—standardized tests, teacher-made tests, portfolios, interviewing, surveys, teacher evaluation throughout the learning process, and so on. Additionally, we need to determine what information our various constituencies need—parents, teachers, students, school board members, and community—and for what purposes.

This leads us to a fruitful discussion on the various kinds of assessment and how they can be used in different ways. Parents who want to understand how their child learns in the classroom prefer to look at the child's portfolio while the child explains how he or she went about the work (Hebert, 1992). Parents who need an occasional outside check to compare their child to other children in the nation want to see results on a standardized test. Some school board members need to be reassured with an outside measure; others prefer to see the results from student portfolios. Principals must determine what form of assessment facilitates the dialogue of what is best for our students. The answer may be quite different at different times.

How we frame our challenges and questions has a major impact on how we think about solutions. Just as we've reframed our assessment question, we've also reconceived the content-versus-thinking skills debate as the challenge to integrate the teaching of thinking and instill a love of learning into the teaching of content. And we've found the question of heterogeneous groups versus homogeneous groups less productive than the question of how best we can teach each child.

We believe that the role of the instructional leader is perhaps one of the greatest challenges of our time. Many factors have public anxiety at an all-time high. People want assurances in the form of accountability, answers, and immediate change. At the same time, the professionalism of our staff is being threatened as decisions are being taken away from them. It is the task of school leaders—not the principal alone—to balance all these needs.

While building public confidence, we must also maintain an environment that tolerates ambiguity, engages faculty in constant critical dialogue, promotes an understanding of all the elements of the context, and encourages making decisions accordingly. This entails constant probing of interactions within the process and how these interactions influence the product we seek. We all need to be learners and to construct theories that make sense. It is certainly not an easy task, but just as certainly it is one that keeps us engaged in constant growth.

Chapter Five

Resources

Balancing Infinite Needs and Finite Resources

Schools seem to run in perpetual arrears. The challenge of addressing every child's learning needs is so immense that, on any given day, an educator, parent, or student advocate can find something that the school could do better for his or her child or student. Typically, principals' offices are the collection points for such somethings. Principals who encourage student and staff growth tend to attract suggestions and ideas for change as a magnet attracts iron filings.

This chapter explores the persisting question: *how can we do all these good things when our resources won't permit us to?* Most good suggestions and ideas never make it beyond the idea stage. Money is short. Technical support and knowledge are insufficient. Teachers, parents, students, and the principal too haven't the time and energy, nor the skills to make it all happen. So the principal is in a permanently delicate position, balanced between wanting to encourage good ideas and new practices and unable to effectuate all of them. Principals are called upon daily to respond to needs that are seemingly infinite in number and variety in a land where resources are decidedly finite.

The diary of Bob McCormick, principal of Pennington Middle School, tells a representative story for exploring this question. We will weave Bob's experiences in and out of our own discussion, questions, and experiences.

October 2

The seventh-grade teaching team took my answer pretty well. They were obviously discouraged that central office rejected their request for discretionary funds to build a hands-on science program about the local environment. But they took it like good soldiers.

October 11

Marie and Penny cornered me in the seventh-grade team meeting space. They want to move away from the science texts we've had for nine years. Their argument makes great sense to me: kids will learn basic natural science concepts a lot better through hands-on activities and by seeing how science works in their own lives. And it fits our middle school mission and philosophy.

October 16

I really got it from the seventh-grade team after school. The non-support for a hands-on science program is stuck in their craw. All six of them came to the office to express their disappointment. Carl even hinted that the administration was welshing on our support for middle school learning, and so soon after we had sent them to a middle school science learning conference this past summer. I told them—for the fourth time—that we just didn't have the resources this year.

October 19

Apparently over the weekend the seventh-grade team met. Marie and Carl were outside my office at 7 A.M.—what a way to start the week. I could feel my blood pressure go up immediately. They pressed their case again, this time saying directly that if we know a better way to teach science, don't we have a moral obligation to put it into action right away?

They gave me a list of budget expense items and suggested we not incur them this year and instead use the money to "support better science for kids," as Carl put it. Their list of items to scratch: new soccer uniforms, renovations to the ceiling on the third floor, two special education–student placements. They also mentioned the principal's contingency fund.

I tried to be open to their suggestion, but I know central office won't support this. We can't just change the budget like that. Dr. Clark doesn't take kindly to pressure from teacher groups. God, I feel caught. The teacher side of me agrees 100 percent with the team. The principal side sees why they just can't go do it.

October 21

I've been thinking a lot about the seventh-grade team's request since Monday. I've hesitated to come right out and argue their case with central office because I'm afraid the superintendent will think I'm not supporting his first decision. Everyone down there will wonder whose team I'm on. But I've also hesitated to go to the team to repeat—for the fifth time—the refusal of their request. When I see any of them in the hall, I feel their eyes on me, waiting for my response.

It's almost come down to a matter of their faith in me as an advocate for kids and for the middle school concept. It's a test of me and my willingness to make things happen for kids. On the other hand, don't I have a responsibility to the district, the administration, and the taxpayers? I mean, we just can't go funding every good idea teachers, coaches, kids, parents, or I come up with, can we?

Can we?

Bob has encouraged the seventh-grade team to be creative and student-centered. He's even sent them to a summer institute. They've come back pumped up, and now they're ready to go. Then stark reality closes in: the school system may not, will not, or cannot immediately provide the resources to support their creative student-centered practices. Their request denied, the teachers are questioning the dedication and good will of the principal and the district.

What started out positive has boomeranged on Bob. As happens to so many principals, he has seen his best efforts to meet the needs of students and staff come face-to-face with the resource limits of the school and the district. Listen in now on Bob's diary from February. In the past week, he's received two documents that pertain to next year's budget. One is a memo from Dr. Clark's office, informing him that Pennington's upcoming annual budget will be reduced from this year's by 3 percent by order of the school board. The second is the seventh-grade team's initial budget request for next year. It contains an itemized list of hands-on science materials and apparatus and a proposal for further summer training for the team.

February 17

I should have seen it coming. The newspapers have been full of cutbacks in other public budgets, so how could I even dream that we would escape it? What really hurts is that I've been encouraging the seventh-grade team to work up that $14,000 proposal for hands-on science since last November. They were so adamant about it—and the thing is I agree with them—that I finally said if they work it up for next year, I'd support sending it to Dr. Clark. Now look at this mess.

February 19

I saw Marie and Carl this afternoon. They asked if the budget proposal they'd submitted was in order. I told them it was and that I appreciated the work they had put into it. I reluctantly had to add the news from Dr. Clark about the 3 percent overall cut for the school. I told them it would be terribly difficult both to make the cut and to go forward with the increases they'd requested, since their request affects only one subject.

Marie went through the roof. She has been the most adamant

proponent of this hands-on curriculum right from the start. What seemed to steam her the most was how much of their own time they'd put into this new curriculum, and now the district was undercutting them. It hurt to hear that. I felt as if she were accusing me of betrayal, as if I'd encouraged them and then dropped them at the most crucial moment.

I did my best to explain that these things at the district level were taking all of us by surprise. She was angry, telling me, "A lot of good that does us. What do you want from us anyway? You make a big deal out of the middle school concept, but we can't get any help to make it go. What's the use of us even trying?" Thank goodness Carl was there, or I would have exploded right back at her.

February 26

I feel as if I hit the wall today. I had a meeting with the seventh-grade team after school. Marie's got them worked up about this budget thing. They sounded almost hopeless: "We've worked hard for Pennington because we believed in the concept, but it's no use the way things are." Marie kept comparing us to Deerfield and the myriad things they have in their middle school.

I do feel as though I've let them down, that I'm personally responsible for their low morale and their anger. I wanted to be a principal because I believed I could be more student-centered than any principal I'd ever worked for. I was tired of living with the shortcomings of administrators. I was ready to show that it was possible to run a school where the needs of kids and the concerns of teachers and parents are listened to.

So here I am. I have a relatively open-door policy. I lead by being involved, staying visible, and accessible. I keep up on new teaching and curriculum methods. I pride myself on knowing every kid's name and knowing as many parents as I can. I enjoy my work with teachers and staff, and I think we have a healthy and open relationship.

What I wasn't prepared for is how they all expect me to solve their problems. I mean, they seem to think I've got the power and influence to make the school over instantly to fit their image of how it should be. I feel like Santa Claus sometimes: everybody's asking me to make our school the happiest and best one yet.

The most discouraging part of this situation is how quickly I've learned to say no. I find myself spending more time explaining why we can't do this or that and explaining the reasons why their good ideas can't come to fruition than I do encouraging them. Rarely do I come flat out and deny a request, because nearly all their ideas have kids at heart.

Maybe Marie's right. Maybe this district isn't a place in which we can have a really good school. Every time I tell myself I might as well be realistic and tell them their ideas can't be accomplished, I know I'm feeding a what's-the-use attitude. Are these teachers—our very best teachers, the ones who care about the kids—beginning to think I don't care?

Do I care?

Principals are caught in a perpetual catch-22. The more good ideas that surface to improve kids' learning, the more principals face requests and demands from caring staff to commit resources to implementing these new practices. The more disgruntled the public and profession are with how we're not meeting the needs of kids, the more new ideas will be advanced for us to try out. Because everybody can be an expert in education, the solutions to our problems come from every quarter. There will always be parents, staff, board members, or local politicians who will support any and all proposals for improvement.

The difficulty comes when we realize we cannot put everyone's ideas into action. Some ideas conflict with one another. Fiscal, technological, and human resources cannot accommodate all good ideas. Bob's tension is not just a budget problem. In fact, we see the money side of the issue as minor when compared to the staff morale and leadership credibility issues. At the crux of the dilemma is Bob's ability to nurture aspirations among teachers, students, and parents; to foster their confidence that the school will do for each child what that child needs; and yet guide their aspirations to be practical enough that the school can deliver on them. In Bob's case, he alone exercises this quintessential function. It is he, as principal, who daily influences the outlook of each participant in the school community: whether they have a sense of hope or one of futility, whether they believe they are performing gainful work or pointless work, whether they feel engaged in productive activity or in mindless routine. As Bob's final diary entry illustrates, a principal's failure to help others realize their aspirations eventually erodes his or her credibility as a leader—with the public, with the staff, and, worst of all, with himself or herself.

How might Bob have handled this situation differently? How might he support the seventh-grade team's efforts, dreams, and faith in Pennington as a good place for kids and for professionals?

Gordy:

My first worry is that Bob has developed a job description for himself that is virtually impossible to live up to. Even if he could, I'd wonder why he wants to. Second, he has framed the immediate problem in such a way that it's very difficult for him or anybody else to solve. He appears to believe that he alone is responsible for nurturing aspirations among teachers, students, and parents—aspirations that are practical enough to meet the needs of each child. That's a lot to ask of himself. The result will become all too familiar: the frustrated overburdened principal, caught between the proverbial rock and the hard place.

Bob's tension is a painful illustration of an occupational hazard. Fullan (1993) cautions principals that "overload fosters dependency" and urges them to move away from the ways in which principals like Bob make themselves responsible for being the master implementors of multiple programs. Fullan asks, "What does a reasonable leader do, faced with impossible tasks?" I would ask Bob the same question.

Let's reframe the problem. What exactly are the external demands on the finite resources Bob controls or influences? The ones he wrote about in his diary appear at first to come from concerned teachers who seek better practices for kids. There's no question that these demands are real, and most principals find these in abundance. They are infinite. They are also inextricably related to the infinite internal demands and expectations Bob places on himself. He apparently believes he should be everything to everyone. I'd ask Bob: why are you, the principal, the only one who is supposed to make good things happen here?

There are a number of reasons why Bob thinks this is mainly his job. First, people who care about children, students, and teachers want a leader who will help them to make good things happen for the kids. Bob McCormick wants to be such a leader. He hears what the seventh-grade team is asking and he agrees with their logic. Their interest in serving kids better is beyond question. Because Bob is a responsive listener and because he agrees to do the best for all students at Pennington, he invites demands on himself and his school.

Bob has conveniently become the kind of leader they want him to be: give me your needs, concerns, problems, and difficulties, and I will take care of them. This is a familiar leadership tension. Bob thinks that people view the principal as a person with the power and influence to make their dreams for the school come true. On the other hand, he realizes he does not singlehandedly have enough power and influence to make everything come to fruition. What are his choices? He runs the risk of undercutting their faith in him if he continues to act as he does. If he changes, he runs the risk of undercutting their faith in him as well. It appears as if he's darned if he does and darned if he doesn't.

Perhaps a way out of this mine field is to be found in what

Bob and others think of as their finite resources. Bob McCormick is clearly in a position of perceived power, sandwiched between what teachers, students, and community want and what central office, voters, and ultimately staff can give. Why can't Bob navigate the shoals between infinite demands and finite resources by keeping staff, parents, upper administration, and students informed of both needs and good ideas and also the real resource limitations. Put simply, if he were to begin to look at some other forms of leadership (Sergiovanni, 1992), he might find that so-called finite resources are not so impoverished. Bob needs to start seeing the resources his constituents can bring to the table. The question becomes: what are the conditions under which the resources that parents, teachers, and central administration have to offer can be utilized as resources? Operating this way, Bob does not have to provide as much direct leadership. Leadership is much less intense and much more informal when issues of control and coordination take care of themselves.

For example, why doesn't Bob share the entire budget process with the staff, thereby sharing the reality and the framework of givens in which they can work together. I get the impression by the number of times that Marie and Carl kept returning that they thought Bob was holding out on them. Clearly, they felt if they were persistent enough, Bob would come up with the money. I would question if Bob hasn't set himself up for this. Perhaps he feels he's not supporting them if he can't come up with the money, and therefore he's reluctant to be definitive.

He and his staff need to get away from the assumption that money is the only expression of support. Perhaps a more useful approach would be to tell them, "The money isn't in the budget, but let's spend some time together looking for other ways we can accomplish the same thing." Most of the materials used in hands-on science classes are found in kitchens, recycling centers, and numerous other resource places. They could make a list of materials they need and send home an appeal to parents in the weekly bulletin. This would promote support as well as a we'll-solve-this-together-as-a-school-community attitude.

Also, there are many publications that list potential grant sources. It is often unfair to ask teachers to take on the extra burden of grant writing, but frequently there are parents who might be looking to develop those skills. In some systems, individuals can get the opportunity to write grants and create a job for themselves. It is important not to fall into the trap of thinking that money is the only way to accomplish change or the only way to express support.

The challenge here for Bob, at a very personal level, is to meet the onslaught of infinite demands by knowing himself well enough to lead personally only those activities in which he is both most needed and most capable of leading. This certainly does not include all activities.

The central question is: if this is an important matter for the school, am I, as principal, the best person to respond to it, and do I have what it takes to respond well? To answer this question, a principal must understand not only the technical nature of school problems and issues but also how people can be brought together to resolve these problems and issues. Against this knowledge base, the principal must judge whether she or he has the skills, time, energy, and patience to lead that effort or whether someone else—or perhaps nobody at all—can take or share the lead.

Richard

Dear Richard:

Thank you for your insightful response to Bob's dilemma. I heartily agree with you that Bob has brought a lot of this upon himself, as a result of his internal demands on himself to be a responsive leader. He is indeed feeling overburdened.

Your suggestions for Bob's next steps make a lot of sense too. If he keeps everyone better informed on both needs and resources, he stands a chance of spreading the burden of matching resources to needs. Your basic suggestion is kind of seductive: that Bob look at some other forms of leadership in which resources are not controlled by the principal but are vested in everybody. I'm not convinced, however, that Bob alone can either (1) teach himself this form of leadership or (2) convince others—for example, those seventh-grade teachers and Dr. Clark—that this new system is a wise one.

Take the second point first. Bob sounds as if he's realistic enough to assess if he's the best person to respond well to each demand that comes his way. Let's say he can make that tough decision and that, for about 50 percent of the demands, he decides he's not the best person. Who does he turn to? He's probably surrounded by good people. If the go-getters on the seventh-grade team are any indication, he's lucky to have creative staff who will give time, energy, imagination, and care to their work— these are their resources. But hasn't he tapped them already? They've been waiting months for him to deliver on the resources that he, as principal, is supposed to deliver: money and a priority on the school's agenda.

Bob's problem is that the environment around him is generally resource-depleted. Perhaps it's more accurate to say that many of the people who populate that environment feel depleted. The problem at this point is to find ways to approach teachers, support staff, central office, parents, local businesses, and others in ways that they don't feel depleted and, quite the opposite, will willingly shoulder a share of the school's burden. To attain this goal, Bob must build a long, solid relationship with all these groups. His effectiveness in doing so will be gauged by his optimism, his openness, and his authenticity on issues of information and power.

Judging from his diary, Bob might not be far off from establishing this relationship with his teachers. It sounds as if they wouldn't be surprised or distressed if he leveled with them about his inability to deliver the goods. I'm not so confident about Dr. Clark, however.

How should Bob approach Dr. Clark to advocate for the science curriculum when Dr. Clark has turned him down several times already? How does he approach teachers, coaches, parents, or support staff and request their help to find resources to get the new program off the ground—especially since they've already had to cut back in their own areas? Unless the staff and community of Pennington Middle School are uncommonly close and uncommonly collaborative to start with, they could be torn apart if he tries to turn this difficult resource reduction-redistribution problem over to them.

If this were to happen, the repercussions for Bob could be serious. This takes me back to point one: how can Bob teach himself this form of shared leadership? Bob works in a world where others want him to make the tough decisions and to exercise his power and control so their agendas can be met. Bob too draws satisfaction from making these decisions and shaping the forces in school toward ends that benefit kids. How is he to give some of this up? Especially, how can he ethically give up some of his power if he knows that it means some of the problems will remain unsolved?

The toughest aspect of the internal change you propose, Richard, is that Bob must come to grips with the finiteness of his own resources as well as those of the school. He's got to balance his idealism and optimism with steely practicality. Bob has to learn, as Flip Wilson once put it, "not to let my mouth write a check that my body can't deliver." He must learn to make the tough assessment of his and the school's capacity to respond. He must involve others in that assessment, and together they must ask themselves: do we have the skills, time, energy, and patience to resolve this problem right now?

Most difficult of all, Bob has to learn that if the answer is no, it's okay. Schools have become repositories for infinite demands, yet they are decidedly finite in their resources. As the principal, Bob can never abdicate his ultimate responsibility: to help the school community balance its felt obligation to do the best for all the kids with its inevitable failure to deliver on that obligation. A leader's job is to help the group see what it can do well and to make sure the group stays focused on doing it—even when, just as inevitably, many will want to do more and different things.

> With finality,
> Gordy

All three of us can relate to Bob's dilemma since we've each experienced the pain and frustration of trying to be all things to all people. We fondly refer to this as the black hole of the principalship.

Paradoxically, this is not an unusual state for leaders who enter the principalship believing strongly in shared leadership. Often this belief is predicated on a desire to create an environment for teachers that is totally supportive, stimulating, and engaging. These principals believe it is their role to encourage teachers to clarify their own beliefs and to make things happen for children. They hope to provide for their teachers what they never had when they were teachers.

There is a danger to this. Just as well-intentioned parents often do, you too, out of the best of intentions, can actually foster a sense of powerlessness by continually solving teachers' problems. By doing this, you prevent them from developing as problem solvers and creators of their own environment. Like Bob, you get into the trap of having everyone look to you for all the answers. This leaves you feeling little control over your surroundings (Heifetz, 1994).

We recommend that you approach every resource decision with the following questions: who should be engaged in balancing these needs with available or future resources? Who must be on board to make this balance work? In our view, the principal's job is to create an environment in which all resources—money, time, and talents—are known to everyone. The principal is a bumblebee, so to speak, in charge of cross-fertilizing the resources and engaging all members of the school community in determining how to allocate those resources most effectively. Resources as well as responsibilities are shared as widely as possible.

We realize that it takes a long time and a lot of effort to develop the necessary relationships and skills among staff to accomplish this. We have worked with many principals who moved in that direction successfully but not without some obstacles along the way. Some principals have formed councils to develop the budget, to set priorities, and to organize the available talents within the community. Some principals use a modified collaborative system. They engage grade-level teams in making decisions as to how money is spent at their level. Some divide the pot equally among staff. Some use a combination approach. There are no easy answers or road maps to sharing responsibilities around the balancing of resources and needs. We'd like to share some considerations that principals have pondered when trying to make sense of the process.

When making decisions about the budget or about budget preparation, you are making decisions far greater than where the resources are to go. In some ways you are sketching out the plot for the story of the school. Your decisions regarding allotment of money, time, and talents broadcast to teachers, students, parents, and community what issues you think are most important and what system of decision making you value. Is it a collaborative method? Are others given leadership? Or will it be done solely by the principal? As with most of the persisting tensions, there is no right or wrong answer and never any finality. It is important for the principal to struggle with decisions in keeping with his or her beliefs about leadership and what's important for the school.

Gordy made reference to the need for Bob to teach himself the new conception of leadership. Our experience has been that moving to shared leadership involves more than learning a new set of skills. It requires a great deal of reflection and soul searching as to what one wants to gain from leadership and how to accomplish it. Leaders must consider both the losses and the gains they will experience as they move to shared leadership. This is different for each individual and must be examined as a part of the process.

By sharing the responsibility for meeting everyone's needs, Bob clearly will lighten his own burden and perhaps will empower all those involved with the school to accomplish more for the students. He will though, in all likelihood, lose the feeling of control he currently has over everything that happens in his building. Many principals struggle with the issue of quality too, wondering: if I give up control, what will I do if things aren't done to my standards? And what do I do if they aren't in sync with my beliefs as to what's right for the children?

Gordy was quick to point out the importance of timing and the pitfalls of moving too quickly into such a process. Clearly, decisions about the budget and the budget process influence everything at the school. It would be disastrous if the budget were put in the hands of staff before a sense of trust and teamwork were established. Similarly, during a time when budget cuts must be made, the process could destroy a sense of team. Once again, judgments need to be made on an ongoing basis about who should be involved in what decisions and when. Whatever those judgements may be, it's critical that they are clearly communicated and explained to all who have a stake in the school.

It's also important to consider the impact of outside forces on the principal's decisions concerning resources and the resourcing process. As we saw, Bob found himself very constrained by the demands of the superintendent and the school board. He chose not to share those constraints and his frustrations with his staff, which led them to believe that he had a choice. Could he have shared the givens with them from the beginning? Would this have removed the potential for mistrust and the feeling of nonsupport? Bob seemed to buy into the superintendent's thinking that there were various sides in relation to the allocation of resources. Could Bob have had a frank discussion with the superintendent? Could he have explained that he sees his role as one who energizes teachers and that in his view, having teachers lobbying for resources to make things happen for students is a good sign? At least Dr. Clark would have had a better understanding of Bob's values and priorities concerning allocation and need for more resources.

How a principal goes about balancing resources with needs determines whether the process creates trust, shared effort, and creative use of resources or whether it telegraphs a message of hierarchy, control from above, lack of support, and mistrust. It is a constant source of tension for principals, who must continually take into consideration what messages they want to convey, what results they want to achieve, and if they will achieve those results by the decisions they have made.

Chapter Six

Change

Fostering Change and
Respecting the Individual

Efforts to change schools often meet with resistance, take longer than expected, affect morale, and require a great deal of time and work. (Sergiovanni, 1992; Fullan, 1993). Nevertheless, conventional wisdom suggests that schools should be able to change and that principals should have something to do with it. We believe, as many do, that principals are essential to the shaping of a school. But our experience has taught us that this is not an easy task. As you set out to change the school, you soon find that others do not agree. The principal faces a major tension between the need for change and the need to respect the individuals in the school. Initiating or responding to changes often leads to a familiar question: *how shall we do things, our way or your way?*

This tension naturally produces a number of issues for principals. The most significant of these is how to advocate for change and at the same time respect the legitimate interests and needs of each person. Join our conversation as we explore this dilemma through the letters of a new principal, Herbert Day. Herb attempted to initiate a number of major reforms at Jefferson High, a large urban high school. Herb's letters, spanning the first half of the year, reveal familiar tensions for a principal entering a new setting whose high hopes for change are humbled by the weight of human events.

October 1
Dear Becky, Gordy, and Richard:

I guess you could say I am enjoying my first principalship, although *enjoy* is probably a strange word to describe the way I'm feeling about this job. I believe I was selected to be principal of Jefferson High School because I promised to bring about what I thought (and they thought) were much-needed changes. I convinced them I was the man to make those changes. It was hard to get a sense of the whole picture when I was first interviewed for the job. The biggest change has turned out to be the reorganization of the high school into smaller units, commonly known as a house system. Let me give you some background.

The public schools in this district serve a changing population of almost twelve thousand students. In the past ten years, linguistic minorities increased from 10 percent to over 50 percent, and the proportion of students performing below the norm on state achievement tests rose to over 80 percent. These shifts have brought public demands for changes in programs, services, and materials. In response, central office officials have intensified efforts to improve educational programs, targeting the high school as the most critical area of need.

Jefferson High has undergone very little organizational, structural, or philosophical change, with tradition and past practices dictating most of its norms and educational policies. We have approximately two thousand students, representing a diverse mixture of languages, cultures, and backgrounds. Many of the problems characteristic of large urban high schools have become increasingly prevalent here during recent years. Truancy, retention, dropout rate, teen pregnancy, drug abuse, as well as crime and violence, are all part of the day-to-day business, which, to varying degrees, affects my staff and students.

My teaching staff and administration consist of a large number of Jefferson graduates, who constantly remind me that I'm an outsider. My teachers are aware of the existing problems. They live with them daily, and I know they are frustrated and increasingly fearful. Some blame the problem on the poor elementary and middle-grade programs within the city schools. My teachers and department heads are adamant in their defense of the quality of the content, methods, and standards of excellence which form the cornerstone of the high school curriculum. In the past they have been left alone by central office as well as by the principal.

I believe the majority of my teachers are hard working and sincere in their efforts to articulate effectively the existing curriculum. Although they are only too aware of the problems, they feel they are doing the best they can to educate their students and believe they shouldn't be held accountable for what they consider outside factors such as student backgrounds, absenteeism, and discipline problems. They see the constant attacks hurled at them by central office administration as unwarranted and unfair, serving only to increase their growing frustration and dissatisfaction.

So I entered just a few months ago (has it only been four months? it feels like five years), promising to do something about everything: the development of a house system, an impending loss of accreditation, the alarming decline in student achievement, the escalating dropout rate, and myriad other problems. The house system seemed to be the key to getting things moving. Knowing that I'm a former house master with a doctorate in educational administration, they were convinced—and I guess I convinced them—I could create a house system, which, as I'm painfully learning, is quite different from running one. I wasn't intimidated by the stories of violence and disciplinary problems. I also thought I was savvy enough politically to understand the undercurrents generated by the existing controversies.

When I began, I was confident in my ability to get the job done. Frankly, now I'm just not so sure. If I had known at the time of my interviews what I know now, I'm not sure I would have taken the job. I'm not even sure anymore what the job is. I suppose the main thing I'm looking for now is some kind of anchor. I feel as if I've been in a hurricane these last few months, and I

haven't known how to stop it. Do I have a choice? Is it presumptu-
ous of me to think I can stop it? I feel as if I'm really losing sight of
what's important.

Sincerely,
Herb

December 1
Dear Richard, Gordy, and Becky:

Things are starting to heat up around here. My efforts to reorganize are facing severe problems, not the least of which is growing
dissension on the part of my administrative staff and teachers. At
the suggestion of the assistant superintendent, I initiated a reorganization process by convening a committee composed of high
school teachers and other personnel, along with representatives
from central office administration and a school board member, to
study the feasibility of reorganizing the high school into a house
system. Meetings have been held regularly, and visits to other districts with house systems have been arranged so that committee
members could study these firsthand.

From the outset, the dynamics within the committee were
charged with reactivity. Although I tried to act as a buffer between
central office officials and high school staff, the committee has
become adamantly divided in its support pro and con of the pend-
ing house system.

The members of the pro group are, unfortunately, in the
minority. Luckily though, they're energetic and share my vision of
a high school that must innovate in order to meet the crying
needs of our students. Two of them, Selena and Doreen, have
already drawn up a plan for one house in which all classes would
be taught in both Spanish and English. They have the support of a
neighborhood committee. What I like about them is that they
have some fire in their gut! Sometimes I wish I could just take
them and start a new school.

The con group looms like a vast gray cloud over me—and over Selena, Doreen, and their cohorts as well. These aren't bad people, but they cannot be convinced that anything can be done about the situation. Some of them keep saying, "No way we'll water down what we're teaching for these kids." Others insist we don't need to reorganize; we just need more English tutors and on-the-job training. Still others threaten that if they are required to work in house teams and subjects, they will protest it as an unnegotiated change in working conditions.

Sometimes, when I'm at my angriest, I think they're all just "lifers" putting in their time until retirement, doing what they've always done, and taking a defeatist view of our chances to make a difference with these kids. Certainly some are like this. But when they protest loudest about my proposals, I hear another voice in there—more like a voice of caution or fear than a voice of disagreement. I think they would really like to make this school work better (I mean, how could they ignore the evidence of Jefferson's terrible failure!). I think they're worried that we'll lose control of everything if we try to change anything. They're sort of a let-sleeping-dogs-lie group.

Discussions have become increasingly ardent, angry, and impassioned. As the disputes have been taken outside the committee room, the effects on my teachers have become even more disastrous. Other staff are taking sides, with heated debates erupting intermittently throughout the school day.

I am constantly reminded of my promise to reorganize the school—a promise repeatedly invoked by school officials during my recurring summonses to the superintendent's office. I confess that for the first time in my professional life, I feel vulnerable, and I realize that my credibility and strength as an educational leader are at stake. My reputation seems to hinge precariously on the successful introduction of the house system. At the same time, I feel that we are going about this all wrong. I know I shouldn't allow my insecurities to surface because this will make me appear weak and will threaten further my already tenuous control of the situation. As the bitter battle continues on, I am becoming more emotional, increasingly entangled within the arguments, and overly reactive; I'm lashing out at teachers for the smallest things.

I feel myself progressively losing ground in my attempts to win over the staff and bring them to collaborative agreement on any outcomes. A few months ago, I was convinced that change was inevitable and imperative to the school's survival as a successful accredited secondary institution, but I am becoming less sure of that. I have the feeling that the entire effort to generate cooperation and collaboration has backfired into the worst disaster I've ever been faced with.

It is a few weeks to the holiday break and I need it. I know that something has to be done and soon. I sense the majority of this staff are starting to view me as the enemy, and open hostility is becoming evident in other ways. Nonetheless, the central office keeps reminding me that the house system is coming. Unless I can conjure up a miracle to turn the tables, it will have to be virtually forced upon the staff. Based on my experience so far, I fear it will come at a great cost. Help!

Herb

We're sure you have recognized between the lines of Herb's letters some of the familiar tensions implicit in the muddy waters of change. It is difficult to be both sensitive and critical of your school. This is due in part to the combined weight of the expectations you encounter, the actions you take, and the initial results of those actions. Principals, by virtue of the leadership positions they hold, attract others' hopes and dreams for change. But that position obligates them as well to consider and often to enact these changes, frequently in concert with others who do not agree with or understand the changes.

The tension for principals is that, as lines get drawn more

deeply in the sand regarding how things should or should not change, they, like Herb, find themselves wondering how to foster change and at the same time respect individual needs and differing positions. Gordy and Becky explore a number of options for Herbert Day to pursue in the light of these familiar tensions.

Dear Becky:

I have just finished reading Herb's letters to us, and I must say I feel defeated just reading them. He is faced with an enormous school, a faculty that knows only the traditional ways, a student population that isn't learning—many not even staying in school—and a superintendent and board that hired him to change it all. I can see why he's losing sleep!

I think Herb may have contributed to the problem somewhat. Here he is, newly hired with a mandate to change Jefferson High. He even said he had convinced the central office and board that, "I was the man to do it." But then what does he do? He forms a committee to study the matter, and suddenly he's deluged with all this anxiety, doubt, and disagreement from his staff. On top of all that, the central administration begins to wonder what's happened to his promise to make it all happen. I'd suggest Herb back up a step and take a new tack with his staff and his committee.

First, let me say that I agree wholeheartedly with Herb and the central office about the house system. Large high schools seldom have worked. We've learned from the Coalition of Essential Schools (Muncey and McQuillan, 1993) and other efforts to personalize high schools that neither students nor staff can feel any control over their learning and their work in schools of Jefferson's size. So Herb should stay the course, but he shouldn't be so faint-hearted about it. He was hired to make change. He came in with a clear idea of what direction that change should take. So why assemble a large committee and study it to death? That's only going to provoke people and raise anxieties about: what's going to happen to me? and in the end the change will take a lot longer. He should cut his losses by asking the large committee to report its major findings regarding the house system right away and then move on to a steering committee composed of no more than seven influential people who can help make the proposal succeed.

Herb should appoint Selena, Doreen, a couple of senior faculty who are levelheaded and widely respected, and an active citizen who can bridge to social service agencies in the city. He also needs to have the assistant superintendent on the committee, or someone else who can make it abundantly clear to everyone that central office and the board want this change to happen and will support it with resources.

Herb should have this steering committee develop a plan for implementing the house system next fall, and they should develop it by mid February, so it can be considered from three crucial viewpoints simultaneously: (1) central office's ability to support it with resources and clout, (2) the community's ability to support it philosophically, and (3) the faculty's ability to put it into effect. In the case of the faculty, I suggest they focus not on *whether* it'll be put into effect but on *how*. I suggest this because the way I read Herb's staff, they're probably most worried about how the house system will work and how it will affect them and their current comfort levels. With a clear plan, the solid support of the leadership and the community, and the promise of some resources to help make it happen, most of the staff will probably come along.

Herb will have to pay closer attention to the politics of his situation than he seems to be doing. Frankly, he's let himself get squeezed by the superintendent and the board on one side and his faculty on the other. He has to remember that the superintendent and board wanted this change in the first place. He needs to stay in close contact with them, to make sure they support his plan, and that they know about the resistance he's getting. They can also be excellent connections to the community and to city government. Herb should spend more time and energy finding out who's who in town and lining up business support and community leadership behind his plan for Jefferson. It's time to show his faculty that the train is already pulling out of the station.

A final note about Herb's staff is necessary. It seems as if he started off by trying "to do the consensus thing." In a school as big and as tough as Jefferson, I'd guess that teachers, counselors, and other staff feel so embattled that they don't want to be consulted. They just want to be led out of this mess. On top of that, they've never had to work together before; the last principal left them to their own devices. To further complicate it, a staff of 118 is far too big for consensus building, at least in the way Herb has approached it. This group needs firmer leadership: a concise proposal, a chance to plan the specifics of putting it in place by June, and a principal whose belief in both the proposal and in them is abundantly obvious to everyone.

Once they're in smaller faculty groupings and Herb has appointed the Selenas and Doreens as house leaders, they'll all begin to see and feel the benefits.

I'd love to be there to see the results myself.

Gordy

Dear Gordy,

I don't know about you, but I found Herbert Day's letter very humbling. Poor Herb was really set up because he went in as an agent for the superintendent's vision. No wonder the staff is resisting him. I know many people who have engaged in making a vision for a school happen, but it has been the staff's vision, not the superintendent's. Even if Herb's vision is similar to the superintendent's, to sell it as the superintendent's is probably not going to assist him.

My advice for any principal entering a school is listen, listen, listen, get to know the staff, and build trust. Basic, but sometimes we get so tied up in vision, beliefs, school reform, and so forth that we forget the basics. Herb is probably not the only principal out there trying to make his or her vision or that of the superintendent happen in the first year.

Herb says that many of his teachers are graduates of the school. I'd start there, by suggesting he take a good look at the rich history of the school. He should have conversations about how Jefferson got to this point and find out about the history, traditions, experiences, and stories of the school. The people in his school—the teachers, parents, staff and students—have some very important ideas that he needs to pay attention to.

He can accomplish a number of significant but not so obvious objectives by doing this:

1. Help people to wean themselves from their intense identification with their positions.

2. Lead people away from a myopic, nonsystemic view of their school.

3. Create a way to acknowledge the contributions, however small, that everyone makes.

4. Move the group toward a larger vision of what they really want for their future and that of their school.

I think that if he starts to look at Jefferson this way, something in him will change. Instead of a person who feels pressure to have all the answers, knowing which directions to take, he'll become a detective trying to find out the important information that all these people have to offer. Once he does that, I think others will want to help determine what actions are necessary for the school to grow into a different and better place.

Part of it will involve his letting go of some issues about his own leadership. Then he can acknowledge that the people at Jefferson have some important answers, stemming from their sense of history and their sense of place about the school. After all, many of their lives have been shaped by this school. I don't see this as an end in itself, but at least his divided staff may find a way to start talking to each other again.

Herb said he didn't want to show his vulnerabilities. I think he would do himself a service by sharing all of himself—vulnerabilities included. Herb keeps referring to the house system as the superintendent's vision. I suspect he too believes intensely in the system and has experienced firsthand its benefits for students as well as some of its pitfalls. I think Herb should share with the entire staff his frustration at not being able to move toward a house system and why he believes in it so strongly. He needs to acknowledge that if others aren't interested in moving in that direction, it's okay—at least for a while. It would be important to ask them to keep their minds open and explore the concept with him. He might encourage this by providing various forums wherein he can share his excitement about the concept. He should encourage staff members to visit other districts that use the house system.

It would probably be to Herb's advantage to meet informally with the superintendent, perhaps over lunch, share his excitement about the progress that has been made with Doreen and Selena, and convince the superintendent that the best way to move to the house system is to start with one house headed by Doreen and Selena—a pilot within the school. He must make it clear that the superintendent's support—in the form of resources, visits, newspaper articles, and presentations to the school board—is key to making the project a success. Herb should be clear that he is not backing away from the concept but has decided to take another tack to assure its success.

People need to feel as though they have control over their lives. Herb hasn't given the staff a chance to ask themselves if they think a house system can benefit their students and their work as teachers. I trust that Herb believes it can and knows the reasons why. He should be confident that if he presents the concept and gives the staff time to understand it, they too will choose it. He needs to convey that the choice is theirs. Then he needs to sell his position. I know he has a far greater chance with this approach than he does of trying to make people a part of the superintendent's vision.

I predict that the excitement this is going to generate will sweep many faculty members off their feet. As they see Doreen and Selena working with other people to develop their vision for the house and see it come to fruition, other faculty members will enthusiastically hop on board. Of course, Herb has another set of problems. How will he decide which teachers and children to be in the house? What about curriculum? Perhaps teachers could be given free rein to design integrated curriculum or even teach just one course at a time. This could all be worked out in the planning.

Herb will have his hands full. But I can't help thinking that Herb would enjoy working with a group of educators asking questions about what's best for students. What he has now is a group of individuals concerned about issues of power and territory.

I too wish I could be there!

> Sincerely,
> Becky

As Becky and Gordy's perspectives suggest, there is never a guarantee that everyone will, or even should be, in total agreement concerning the value of a particular change, whether it involves the fundamental restructuring of a school or a modification in cafeteria duty for teachers. The principal's challenge is not to forge total agreement. Rather, it is to find ways of creatively harnessing the energy created by the tension of advocating for change while respecting the legitimate interests and needs of each person.

We see a number of potentially useful ways for principals to navigate the turbulent waters of change. First, we think principals need to examine critically their expectations of themselves by taking an honest look at the values that guide their leadership behavior. Second, principals should learn how to engage others in the process of considering both what should change and why things should change.

Many principals, like Herb, find themselves unduly influenced not only by circumstances but also by the conceptions and ideas of leadership they hold (Fullan, 1993). For example, Herb brought to Jefferson High an idea of leadership familiar to many. It is one that assumes principals can, by their will, impose order and rationality on what is otherwise unordered chaos. Herb says he applied for his job and won it because he believed he could get the job done, and he convinced others of it. In doing so, he naturally had to live up to an image and expectation of his own leadership that, at least in part, he had created for himself.

We believe that before principals envision or mandate changes for others, they benefit from looking at and understanding how their own expectations of themselves as leaders may help or hinder their leadership in action. Principals can create this kind of self-knowledge through consistent and authentic reflection on their leadership practices (Schön, 1983). An example of reflection we've found useful is to consider a scenario that we'll call the "best kind of situation." Recall a time when you were in a predicament similar to Herbert Day's at Jefferson High School. Think of a situation that involved uncertainty and conflict, when you felt off balance in the way Herb does—perhaps an experience, a conversation, or an encounter with a colleague or adversary—and you felt conflicting expectations about what you were doing as a leader. Recall observable feelings and behaviors, what you did and how you reacted to circumstances, rather than what you thought you should have done. We think these moments are the best times, albeit the most difficult, to see how your assumptions about your own leadership collide with reality. The idea is to bring to the surface and to expose your own expectations of your leadership for you—and perhaps for others—to see.

This kind of reflection, we have found, leads to a more realistic assessment and understanding of who you are and what you do as a leader. (Appendix B suggests an approach to this kind of self-assessment.) A colleague shared some of his own hard-learned leadership principles, a result of a number of situations from which he'd accumulated, as had Herb, some battle scars. We'd like to share them with you.

My Personal Leadership Principles

1. I will be more productive, in many situations, if I bring my own self/reasons/beliefs/vision to the interaction than to remain faceless, even if that means being negative.

2. I should not attribute ineffectiveness in the school to my own incompetence; everything is not my fault.

3. I do not have to be perfect.

4. I can assume different roles, including authoritative ones, and still be congruent with my vision of collaboration and dialogue.

5. I must attend to my own needs—self care, survival, peace of mind—as they are more important than the act of leadership itself.

6. I should confront conflicts that address issues of trust, collaboration, teamwork, and my own well-being.

7. I am fine, and I'm a competent and a good person even if some people don't like me or don't like what I'm doing (Elliot Stern, 1992).

We believe his articulation of these principles signals his ability to see his school staff for who they are, not who he needs them to be.

Remember Herbert Day's final words? Considering the prospective effect of the change he wanted to bring about, he thought, "Based on my experience so far, I fear it will come at a great cost."

These words express considerable self-doubt about his ability to manage what has quickly become a series of messy changes for Jefferson High School. We see his honest self-acknowledgment as a blessing rather than a curse because it signals Herb's first awareness of needing to listen to the people and the community of Jefferson High School. He realizes that he alone does not have all the answers, and he is getting beyond seeing things as he would like them to be and beginning to see them as they are. This is Herb's work at Jefferson.

We don't want to suggest that managing your own expectations of yourself as a leader will alter the fact that others have significant expectations of you. The question of course is: what do you want to do about that? Gordy suggests that Herb may have contributed to the problem by taking his mandate to introduce the house system from the central office and then forming a committee to study the matter, thereby creating anxiety, doubt, and disagreement within his staff as well as within the central office. Becky suggests that Herb was never on firm footing to begin with because he went in as an agent for the superintendent's vision, not the staff's vision.

How do principals like Herb determine a course: one that honors the legitimate interests of all stakeholders, acknowledges the real conflicts inherent in different positions, and gets the work done effectively? Gordy's and Becky's perspectives both focus on a commitment to a process through which Herbert Day might be able to bring changes to Jefferson High. The steps they propose for Herb differ, but their goals for him are similar. Perhaps the real work for Herb is instituting a process that engages others in the work of changing the school and doing so on their own terms. Easier said than done, we say.

Some would probably argue that Herb exercised good management and leadership judgment in his attempts to convene a representative committee to consider the development of a house system at Jefferson. This strategy seems to make sense by today's standards where shared leadership and decision making are considered so important. Yet, others rightfully counter that the pressure of time is one of the most insistent on principals, especially when it comes to decisions and change. There is never enough time to involve everyone and to obtain everyone's input. Many principals find themselves exercising a high degree of authority with little time for delegation to others.

The sides have formed at Jefferson High, and all those involved have had time to dig their trenches. There is conflict and genuine disagreement. If you follow the logic of the position Gordy has taken, it essentially comes down to "my way or else," a view that reflects a popular and conventional wisdom of change. Principals are reminded from all quarters that they should have a vision of the future for their organization. These days, it has become a reflex for principals in situations requiring change to set the course, formulate the vision, and then get as many true believers on board as possible. Although this position sometimes brings about immediate change, it often takes a long-term toll on human interaction, involvement, and commitment, which is deleterious to lasting change. In fact, we think true change ultimately must focus on improvement in student learning. It is unlikely that any such long-lasting change will occur without the involvement of the entire school community.

This does not mean that everyone must agree. Reasonable people will agree to disagree. Values can and will clash (Berlin, 1990). We view the question "Our way or your way?" as the beginning of a conversation that is necessary to help members of a community "come to *their* vision." The struggle around the question can be a fruitful one. Out of the process can evolve a sense of ownership, passion, a willingness to commit and to put one's beliefs out for public scrutiny. Principals face the challenge of helping each person clarify his or her way and to articulate it to others. If each person's way is visible, a true conversation can begin about the creation of "our way."

Chapter Seven

Ownership

Weaving Diverse Interests into Mutual Purpose

Research tells us that schools that embrace shared decision making and collaboration produce better results for students (Joyce and Showers, 1995; Little, 1982). Common sense tells us that schools function better when the adults invested in them work well together. Ideally, if all constituencies cooperated, our schools would thrive. Though this is clearly not the case in many communities, the expectation that it should be falls squarely at the feet of the principal.

Any school leader who has struggled to build shared decision making and broad-based collaboration knows that the process of putting them into practice is slow and painful. The struggle toward these laudable goals invites wide participation from educators, parents, community officials, and governmental and volunteer organizations. With this participation comes a numbing array of goals, ideologies, beliefs about learning and child rearing, and personalities. The principal, positioned at the school's public threshold, is facilitator, sense maker, diplomat, mediator, and much more.

This chapter explores a basic tension over ownership: how can we respond to the needs of individual constituencies while also building·and maintaining a unified direction for the school as a whole? Let's listen to Sherrie, the principal of the Horace Mann School, as she struggles with a number of tensions underlying the challenge of sharing leadership in a school. Sherrie is sitting in her office, gazing at a plaque on the wall, titled "My Vision." Her family had this engraved for her when she received her graduate degree.

I remember when I took this job. I had already spent so much time working in schools, studying schools. I was so certain I knew what should happen to improve schools and so convinced I could make it happen. I even remember one of my last papers in graduate school, "My School Vision." And here I have on my wall the four key ideas expressed in that paper that seemed like pure common sense to me.

- All the people in the school should be involved in decisions that affect their lives.
- Many constituencies—teachers, custodians, specialists, parents, secretary—should make decisions. Collectively reached decisions are stronger and will be owned by all constituencies in the implementation phase.
- Students benefit when adults model what they want for students: a love of learning, a sense of empowerment, critical thinking, and creative problem solving.
- Schools should be organized so that each individual has the opportunity to realize his or her own vision and beliefs.

Six years later, I'm more committed to my beliefs than ever and also more aware of the struggles one encounters in trying to live by them.

I've had my share of bruises to prove it. I remember my first awakening to parent involvement, which came during my first year at Horace. I believed so strongly that parent involvement is a key component to children's success. I immediately set up a parent forum consisting of eight representative parents who met with me regularly to help identify problems and brainstorm solutions. It seemed to be running very smoothly. Other parents in the school community called the representatives with their concerns; we addressed them, and I really thought we were building a true sense of team. It wasn't until an issue exploded that I learned the complexities of parent involvement. It was the nightmare of nightmares for all principals: a playground incident.

I vividly remember the first hint of disaster. It was 5 P.M. and the phone rang. Judy had gone for the day so I casually picked it up with a cheery, "Horace Mann School. May I help you?"

On the other end of the line, I heard an outraged and practically incoherent person. "You better be prepared for the lawsuit of your life. This is Mrs. Wright and I'm going to have your head!"

Somewhat taken aback, I managed to pull myself together, and with a false calm answered, "Please, Mrs. Wright, tell me what's wrong. I'm sure we can work it out."

"Well, my son Frank was at the bottom of a pile of eight children during recess today, and his arm was almost broken. The instigator was a kid named Tommy. This kid shouldn't even be in a public school!"

I tried to respond to her as calmly and quietly as I could: "Unfortunately, Mrs. Wright, this is the first I'm hearing about this incident, and everyone has already gone home. Please give me a chance to look into it in the morning, and I promise to get back to you as soon as I can. How is Frank? Is he all right?"

"He's okay. But no thanks to you or your school. I expect immediate action. If I don't get it, I'll have your job!"

I put down the phone, shaken and perplexed. I hadn't heard a thing about the incident. Incidents of this severity were rare at Horace, and I usually heard about them immediately.

The next morning I spoke with Frank's teacher before the children arrived. She thought the mother must have been referring to something that had happened at lunch recess with the lunchroom aides. Apparently, Frank had approached Mrs. Bowman and told her that Tommy had thrown him on the ground. Mrs. Bowman asked Frank if he wanted to go to the nurse, but he said he felt fine. The teacher also informed me that Frank did not even looked rumpled, that he had a tendency to exaggerate about things anyway, and that she had not taken the incident very seriously.

I was returning to my office when I came face to face with Frank and his father. "I assume the situation has been taken care of," he bellowed at me. I told him I was looking into it. He retorted, "I don't see that there's any looking into. Tommy should be suspended. In fact, he should be sent to another school." I invited Mr. Wright into my office and suggested that Frank go right to his classroom. He declined my offer to talk and said he'd call later in the day to see what I'd done.

I spent the morning talking to any staff and students who could possibly shed some light on the incident. The consensus seemed to be that it hadn't been that big a deal. In fact, in a meeting with Frank and the other children, Frank himself agreed that it wasn't a big deal and thought the problem was over.

I called Mr. Wright and began to explain how I had resolved the issue. He angrily snapped at me, "You had no right to involve my son in a discussion, especially with Tommy, and now you're calling him a liar. This is harassment and you're going to pay for this."

That afternoon, I received a phone call from the superintendent of schools, who asked me to explore the severity of the "playground problem" at Horace. His tone indicated that he accepted the problem as a given. Obviously Mrs. Wright had already called him. I started to explain the situation, but then I realized that I was sounding extremely defensive. I concluded the conversation by assuring him I would explore the playground problem.

Later that afternoon, I received a phone call from a supportive parent, who was outraged on my behalf. She wanted me to know that Mrs. Wright was calling parents to form a group to demand that Tommy be put out of school. Sure enough, I got phone calls registering concern about the dangerous child in the third grade and urging me to take action. I felt I couldn't say anything except that I was on top of the situation.

I couldn't figure out any proactive move, so I decided to give the incident some time and just see what would happen. I figured: I had enough credibility; Horace Mann had a good reputation for discipline; Tommy was getting the proper services, and I had put out the word to staff to watch out for Frank at recess, so he wouldn't get hurt or harassed.

The following morning I greeted the students as they came in the building. When I went back to my office, I saw every parent from the Parent Forum standing there. It was not their usual practice to come in unannounced, and we didn't have a scheduled meeting, so I knew they must have some serious concern. As I invited them in, I noticed some unusual body language, and then one of them announced that we needed to address the playground problem.

I stayed calm on the outside, but I confess to a momentary lapse of commitment to parental involvement and a desire to flee. I felt as though my hands were tied. Here were people who felt they had a real stake in the school and a real say in how issues were handled. But I could not share information with them as I do with other professionals. I couldn't tell them that Frank had social problems, and we were planning to work on them. I certainly couldn't tell them that Tommy had special needs, that his parents were seeing a counselor, and that we were providing extra services for him. I suddenly realized that I had let parents believe they were part of running the school in the same way that the teachers and the principal are. Yet I couldn't share all of the data with them. I assured them that in the short term I would be out on the playground for every recess, and I would get back to them when I decided how to tackle the issue. As they left my office, a few of them offered to help monitor the playground. They informed me that several neighbors had invited friends to watch over the fence to see how things really were during recess. I couldn't believe it.

I thought, now you've done it, Sherrie! I thought about those teachers who were just barely tolerating my view that parents should be heavily involved in the school. Some of their comments came back to me: "The next thing you know, they're going to be running the school, and telling us what to do. Aren't we the professionals here?"

I also thought back to the morning meeting with the parents.

We hadn't really worked collaboratively to address this concern as we had done in the past. Truthfully, I felt as if I were being attacked. I spent most of my energies protecting myself, Tommy, and the school. The wall was going up and I was contributing to it.

Despite the feeling of sinking into quicksand, I still believed there was a constructive way for parents to be involved in the process without usurping the role of the staff or taking away their sense of control. I decided to present the situation honestly to the staff at the faculty meeting the next day.

As a faculty, we had decided to put trivial management details in writing and to deal only with meaningful educational issues at our meetings. At the end of each meeting, the faculty built the agenda for the next meeting. I asked them if they'd be willing to add the playground issue to the agenda for the upcoming meeting. They agreed readily, which made me think there had already been a great deal of discussion about it.

At the meeting, I explained the situation as clearly as I could without using names. I admitted that I'd told the parent forum I would provide an opportunity for parents to address the playground problem. At first, I received a lot of emotional reaction.

Susan immediately and vehemently retorted, "We don't have a playground problem, and I resent people saying we do."

Ellen, who was generally supportive of responding to parental concerns, piped up, "This whole problem was caused by a student who has a social problem and we can't control that."

And then the inevitable, "What else would you expect from those forum parents who think they really run the school?"

Jane responded in her usually supportive fashion, "If there's a perception we have a playground problem, then we need to address it."

Slowly the discussion turned to the brainstorming of possible options. The possibilities seemed to fall into three categories: ignore the parents, have a public forum on the playground, or confront the parents and inform them that it's our business and not theirs. To this day, I still mull over those possibilities in my head.

Sherrie's story illustrates the difficulty of involving everyone in a school—parents, teachers, and principals—in the decisions that affect their lives. What can principals do to prevent such trickles from becoming waterfalls? The playground incident reveals the complexity of resolving differences of opinion among key constituents and the monumental task of trying to find a *win-win* solution. The story demonstrates the difficulty of having everyone take part in a decision. It reveals that representative decision making can often fall apart even though it seems great in theory.

How does a principal foster an environment that promotes thinking, love of learning, and empowerment for children and at the same time, use the inevitable tensions that arise among adults as production partners? Is it possible to help constituencies such as parents and teachers tap into their own visions when for years they've believed they couldn't make things happen? And how can a principal reconcile and coordinate the many different visions within a building?

Gordy and Becky next share letters about the dilemma.

Dear Becky:

As I read and reread Sherrie's story, I find myself mulling over the same possibilities that poor ol' Sherrie is probably still mulling over wherever she is. I share her desire to involve parents in school affairs because I believe our partnership with them can help kids' education. I agree too that teachers should come directly in touch with parents so that the vital team of parent and teacher can work directly for kids' benefits. In general, I advocate not protecting the various constituencies of our school—parents, kids, educators, state and federal agencies—from one another. As you can imagine, this didn't make me a popular principal with all my faculty members.

But I differ from Sherrie in a couple of respects. And these, I think, may help her to resolve the dilemma she faces—stuck between potentially warring constituencies. I think she's led parents to think they have a legitimate say over all aspects of the school. She may have given teachers the impression that they do too. If I were her, I'd immediately start to establish clearer boundaries about who has a say over what—and to what extent. I'd try to draw two kinds of lines:

- One line that limits the types of decisions people can have a hand in
- A second line that defines the extent of their involvement

This means that I'd have a talk with each individual—from Mr. Wright to the superintendent—and each group that is active in this episode to clarify legitimate responsibilities. I may feel as though I were trying to corral some cows that had bolted from the barn, and it would take a while to do this, but I think it must be done.

Here is my rationale for the first kind of line I'd draw: I believe that parents' involvement in school should be centered around the education of their own child or children. Where Frank is concerned, Mr. and Mrs. Wright need an open door—to express concerns, make suggestions, listen to suggestions, and carry their share of the load of Frank's education. Notice I don't say they should have a blank check to rewrite school policy, curriculum, or programs for other kids.

When the Mr. Wrights of the community (and the posse of parents that formed) want to run other parents' kids off the playground or out of classrooms, I draw the line. I believe we need to listen to concerns that parents have about other kids, but I don't believe they should have a direct hand in decisions about those kids. This is our territory—and the territory of those kids' parents. I'd call the Wrights and ask for a meeting with them right away. I'd then reset the boundary for them and the pressure group they're forming by explaining the playground-control options we're pursuing and indicating that the matter will be handled by the school staff.

By the way, I'd make this argument for other constituencies too—including teachers. Each person's right to participate in decisions at school is legitimate within his or her own sphere of responsibility. Teachers take an active hand in decisions affecting their students, their teaching team or department, the materials and supplies that affect their ability to succeed most directly. The school board or parent forum share in decisions that fit their responsibilities: policy, fiscal, and management issues, and those activities for which the forum was formed. In clarifying boundaries, I'd reassure teachers that the faculty will make final decisions about the playground and that we'll all be responsible for carrying them out well. I might even call the superintendent and let him know that, while I appreciate his concern about the playground, I consider it our responsibility to respond to the need, not his or the board's.

The other line I'd draw deals not only with the types of decisions parents or others can be involved in but also how far their involvement extends. In general, I would strenuously protect each constituent's right to make final decisions in his or her sphere of responsibility. Parent groups are not ultimately responsible for teaching kids math or advanced biology; teachers are. Teachers are not ultimately responsible for a child's honesty or cleanliness; the parent is. The school board is not ultimately responsible for how French or reading are taught; educators are. The state is not ultimately responsible for whether . . . You get the message.

This sets up what I see as levels of involvement. Saphier presents this as degrees of decision making: informational involvement, consultation/advisement, shared decisions, individual decision (Saphier, Bigda-Peyton, and Pierson, 1989). It seems to me that Sherrie's mistake was that she responded to every person and group in the same way by welcoming them and their input indiscriminately. So she had all sorts of people breathing down her neck and eventually her teachers' necks. The net result was that she ended up stuffing her fingers—sometimes defensively and under great stress—in holes that kept springing up in the dike.

If I were Sherrie, I'd begin right away to clarify for teachers and parents alike the boundaries of their involvement in one another's territory. Mr. Wright would have no business demanding that anything be done with another parent's child. Susan—who resented parents saying we have a playground problem—would need to understand that parents have a legitimate right to inform us if they fear for their children's safety on our playground. I'd welcome the forum parents' concerns about the playground, but I'd carefully draw the line at their "consulting" us. I'd probably thank those parents for volunteering to help on the playground but turn down their offer as well.

I think Sherrie needs to be more a "fence minder" than a "gate opener." Her experience in this case shows us how opening doors to lots of participation can lead to range wars and a kind of wild west atmosphere. That breeds defensiveness and hard feelings, which ultimately detract from everyone's work with children—especially the specific children that belong to their care. If I were Sherrie, I'd do less brainstorming of solutions with these various groups and more outlining of spheres of legitimate responsibility.

> Yours,
> Gordy

Dear Gordy:

What a reaction I've had to your thoughts on Sherrie's plight! As usual you've made me think about myself as a leader and the leader's role in shared leadership. Let me begin by offering what I'd do if I were Sherrie. I'm not entirely clear yet; I'd love to have a long conversation with you to help clarify my thoughts.

If I were Sherrie, I would plan an evening meeting for staff and parents. I would frame the evening as another opportunity to work together to make Horace Mann School a better place for students. I would orchestrate the evening around two assumptions: that any playground can improve and that our purpose is to brainstorm ways to improve ours.

Prior to the meeting, I would work with the parent forum to clarify the purpose of the meeting, to enlist their assistance in sending invitations, and to arrange for their help at the meeting.

Before the meeting, I would assure teachers that they need not be defensive about the playground. Every playground can be improved, and I would try to convince them that it serves us well to approach it that way. I would assure the teachers that they will not be subjected to attack and that I will keep the meeting positive.

In the meantime, I would work individually with the Wrights, counseling on their son's specific needs. And of course, I'd have to be very visible on the playground—partly to assure everyone that there is nothing to be concerned about and partly to see for myself what procedures are used and if there are indeed any problems.

I would open the meeting something like this:

Sherrie: Good evening. Before we begin, I'd like to take a minute to express how fortunate I feel to be principal of a school in which parents and teachers are willing to work together to make this a better place. We have accomplished so much already. Look at this art gallery—just one example of the unique opportunities we've provided our students. My hope for this evening is that we leave here with a plan to make our playground a better and more exciting place for students. I would first like to review a problem-solving process that I've found useful both personally and within groups.

At this point, I'd write the problem-solving steps on the board and describe each one.

Define the problem

Brainstorm solutions

Define criteria for choosing solutions

Develop an implementation plan

Define success

> *Sherrie:* Because so many of us are here this evening, I suggest we stay on task by following these steps:

- Out of respect for our children, we can't discuss individual cases.
- Everyone will be heard.
- All ideas will be considered.

If we went astray, I'd point us back to the board.
With so many heads in one room, some very creative ideas would likely emerge for making the playground better for our students. At the very least, everyone would have an opportunity to provide input and would therefore own the solutions. Both teachers and parents would have a tremendous investment in the work we're doing together. It is important to implement any suggestions that evoke agreement.

Gordy, I know this approach is risky. I have so many questions at this point about shared leadership. It was much clearer to me several years ago. This is true partly because I wasn't so deeply immersed in it then and also because times have changed. People bring very different expectations to a school community than they did just a decade ago.

I'm afraid I have a tendency to walk right into the unknown with some sort of unguarded belief that if we have the opportunity to discuss things in depth among different constituencies, we can find a win-win solution. And you're right; I frequently don't set clear boundaries. To me boundaries signal territory, and I believe that territory and control should not be an issue in relation to children. What's important is listening to and understanding one another's perspectives and at all times keeping an eye on what's best for children. My role as leader is to provide forums and to facilitate the conversation. Isn't this the essence of democracy and what we should model for students?

This approach seemed to work for me, but I must confess things have changed (or maybe I have), and your ideas on setting parameters are intriguing to me. When I first read your letter, my reaction was: come on, Gordy; it's so easy to see roles as clear-cut, and it's so easy to develop a framework on the different levels of decision making when you're sitting in a university. Things never work that way in the real world of schools. I couldn't begin to define where all the different boundaries are.

Maybe part of my problem is that I see most things organically: everything connected to everything else. You suggest that teachers take an active hand in decisions affecting their students, their teaching, or their department. I've tried to instill in faculty that everything they do affects everyone else, encouraging them to think through the impact of their actions on others. Isn't that the definition of community?

When you talk about setting boundaries, the notion is far more intriguing to me than it was just five years ago. Things have changed so much, and parents approach the schools with a very different view. Just a decade ago, we had a handful of parents who participated in evening meetings. Now we have parent advisory councils that are involved in things all the way from curriculum development to the hiring and firing of principals. Sometimes I feel like the principal is left at the mercy of both the composition of the parent group and the expectations each brings to school.

Your comment, "Sherrie . . . wherever she is" hit me hard. I couldn't help but translate it into, where is Becky? I've struggled for years with the question: where is the principal in shared leadership? I used to think the principal was the facilitator of others: teachers, parents, superintendent, community. This meant listening to everyone's vision, weaving their visions together, and supporting them in bringing their visions to fruition, thereby developing many leaders within the community. This way meant spending a great deal more time than with a more authoritarian approach, but in the long run, everyone felt a part of the process and very much alive.

I knew the answer to the question: where am I in all of this? I was facilitating a process I believe in: that each individual has something significant to offer and will unleash tremendous energies when provided the opportunity.

It's much more difficult to do this now. Any leader must constantly ask: how do I change with the times? The relief I felt when you discussed setting parameters leaves me with many questions, theoretical as well as personal. If times have changed such that I need to begin setting parameters, do I have the skills to do it? Do I believe in it? Was I able to involve everyone in the past because it was easy then, and am I giving up my beliefs just because it is more difficult now?

Yours,
Becky

How do principals like Sherrie respectfully tap the resources of well-intentioned parents and teachers? How can parents and teachers be involved in school affairs so that everyone who wants a responsible role gets the information and the authority to exercise that responsibility legitimately? Sherrie's story provides an insider's view of some murky dilemmas for principals, parents, and teachers when the door to participation is opened wide.

We will revisit Becky and Gordy's conversation and explore some pathways for sharing leadership. We will also suggest some ways for you to consider sharing your leadership.

The positions that Gordy and Becky have staked out actually aren't as far apart as they seem. Each makes implicit assumptions about the degree to which Sherrie can control and influence the situation. Gordy suggests that Sherrie can control matters—implying they are controllable—by drawing lines to limit the types of decisions each group can participate in and defining the extent of their involvement. Becky assumes that Sherrie's influence, charisma, and facilitation skills can control and hold things together. As Sherrie says, "I'm afraid I have a tendency to walk right into the unknown with some sort of unguarded belief that if we have the opportunity to discuss things in depth among different constituencies, we can find a win-win solution." Both Gordy and Becky have faith that Sherrie can find her win-win. They just have defined the means somewhat differently.

Underlying both Gordy and Becky's perspectives are a number of assumptions about constituents' interests, needs, rights, and responsibilities and the principal's level of control, power, and influence over these. Gordy doubts that all participants have all students' interests at heart. He commits Sherrie to a decision-making process that limits the respective turf and authority of parents and teachers. He assumes that these artificial boundaries will keep apart extraneous forces, competing demands, and outside pressures—all threats to a logical decision-making process (Patterson, Purkey, and Parker, 1986). Gordy sees Sherrie's situation as a kind of hegemony in which power and responsibility are finite, and her job as leader is to apportion them equally to keep things balanced.

Becky's view invests more faith in the ultimate altruism of teachers and parents. She believes that a decision-making process must accommodate various and sometimes even competing points of view, inevitably leading to a win-win. Becky sees an organic process and prefers not to view power as finite. She believes in working with parents and teachers to create more power, having faith that things will work out in the best interests of children. Becky views her role as leader as one who provides forums and facilitates conversation, thus ensuring a process that will lead to a resolution of the playground incident.

Gordy believes that if the parts are defined carefully and orchestrated firmly by the principal, the whole will come together. Becky believes that the whole is greater than the sum of its parts. Both perspectives acknowledge the complex web of interrelationships and subtle interconnections between parents, teachers, and principal.

Research is remarkably consistent on this point: the principalship is highly interpersonal, full of ambiguity and conflicting expectations. Principals face a diverse range of problems beyond their direct influence (Greenfield, 1982). We believe that the new work of principals is to look at wholes and parts at the same time (Senge, 1990b). Leaders must look at the systems (Senge, 1990a) in which playground incidents arise and understand the subtle patterns of human events that give each school its unique character and culture.

Given the fluid milieus in which principals are supposed to share decisions, collaborate, and share leadership, we suggest a number of avenues for Sherrie and other principals to consider:

1. Revisit where she stands and consider her own role in sharing leadership within the school.

2. Examine assumptions about other people's roles and interests, and examine the legitimacy of these assumptions.

3. Find ways to help others identify, clarify, and articulate their competing interests and values and the problems these conflicting interests create for everybody.

We believe that sharing leadership in this sense means sharing not only the solutions but also the conflicts, issues, and problems that accompany leading. In the final analysis, the principal must help others to define their problems, take responsibility for them, and whenever possible, solve them (Heifetz, 1994).

We see principals as fallible humans faced with an enormous number of issues related to the control, coordination, and efficacy of an organization. The principal may not always be the best person to resolve each issue. We suspect that the ability to discern when it is best to throw off the "burdens of presumed competence" (Barth, 1990) may be the first step toward legitimately sharing leadership.

Becky asks: where am I in all of this? We hope that the many possible answers to this important question will steer principals away from traditional conceptions of their roles and responsibilities. Roles based on control, power, and influence, which are inherited from industrial models of leadership (Rost, 1991), fail in today's world, which doesn't easily accord that degree of control, power, or influence. We suggest you consider your own core beliefs about sharing leadership within a school, rerun the case of Sherrie in your mind, and put yourself in her shoes. What would you have done on the telephone with Mrs. Wright? When confronted with Mr. Wright in the hallway? When you found the members of the parent forum in your office? When you were at the faculty meeting?

This will engage you in exploring your assumptions about other people's interests and the legitimacy of those interests. How does a principal identify the valid interests of constituents? We think that a critical step in achieving shared leadership is to determine first your own assumptions about the needs and interests of others. Then test your assumptions.

How do I, as a leader, help to mobilize people to clarify, articulate, and perhaps solve the problems that result from competing values (Heifetz and Sinder, 1988)? The playground incident and incidents like it are nested in a larger web of needs, interests, and values. We believe that school leadership requires knowledge of the interrelationship among all these parts, but we don't think this knowledge should be the sole domain of the principal. We see principals' work as not only seeing the interrelationships but also helping others to see them.

This approach determines a very different direction for principals' work: not to use their authority to limit other people's spheres of decision making or even to bring a group to consensus but rather to facilitate in a noncoercive way the development of mutual purposes (Rost, 1991). This leads to a different view of Sherrie's role and a different interpretation of such ideas as shared decision making, teacher leadership, and collaboration. Rather than adopting the position that a principal knows best, this view requires the principal to enable everyone to examine carefully the many competing adult interests within a school, to determine collectively what issues and problems are to be solved, and to assess how to mobilize their own group resources to solve those problems (Heifetz and Sinder, 1988).

Chapter Eight

Autonomy

Encouraging Creativity and Preserving Community

All three of us became principals because we saw in the role the potential to free teachers from bureaucratic fetters. As teachers, we felt confined by the routines and the regulations of our schools. We saw in ourselves and our colleagues the potential to teach more creatively and to solve many schoolwide challenges more sensitively and effectively than administration alone could. We felt, by becoming principals, we could unleash in our teachers the capacities and skills for both individual and collective leadership.

Not so simple, we have found. Some teachers welcomed our overtures of trust and encouragement. Others took a long time to overcome the distrust and fear built up over years. Some never did, preferring instead the safety and predictability of the job they originally contracted to do. Still others were offended by the initiatives and the growing influence of their colleagues who had taken the lead.

In short, principals who seek to empower teachers by encouraging their leadership are apt to find that they risk fragmenting the staff and, possibly, causing internal conflict. In addition, these principals must balance the conflicting needs and demands of creative hardworking staff who advocate for different but equally valuable programs. They encounter as well conflicting preferences and goals between teachers who have found their leadership voices and the central office, the school board, and parents' groups. Encouraging teachers to play a greater leadership role throws more balls into the principal's juggling act, which is to incorporate smoothly everybody's involvement in running the school. This leads to our last persisting question: *how do principals balance teacher autonomy with the need to maintain a sense of community within the school?*

Pam is principal of Currier Elementary School. She is deeply immersed in the process of balancing the needs of teachers who have taken on leadership roles. One of the vehicles that Pam has initiated is having teachers write in journals about their visions for the school and their projects. All staff members have agreed to write in their journals on a regular basis with the option of sharing their entries with one another or with Pam. They also have the option of requesting a response.

Pam has found this a very effective way to communicate with staff. She reads journals in the evenings and finds that some staff are more comfortable writing things to her than they are telling her in person. Reading the journals in the quiet of the evening gives Pam an opportunity to think through her responses reflectively and to respond to requests that she couldn't get to during the day. Pam writes in her own journal following each journal-reading session. She has just read Martha and Frank's current reflections and has found the two teachers at odds with one another. Pam then reflects in her own journal:

> At times, it is painful to learn how teachers feel, but it's so important for me to know what's going on if I'm to help work through the conflicts. And boy do I have one now! When I began at Currier, I thought I'd have a difficult time encouraging teachers to take leadership roles. I believe so strongly that my role as principal is to help others sort out their visions and to help them realize these visions. Little did I know how difficult it would be to orchestrate all of the energy that gets unleashed. Most days I feel as if I have a group of thoroughbreds in the building, and my only hope is to attempt to keep them on the same track.
>
> I have so many questions about balancing each teacher's vision with a schoolwide vision. What do I do when I've encouraged two teachers to pursue their dreams, and they end up running head-on

into each other? I've got a real mess on my hands right now with Martha and Frank.

I still remember when Martha came to Currier. I knew she was a leader the day I met her. She is one of those people who can take on anything and do it despite everyone else's doubts. A simple mention of a famous local artist's paintings, for example, prompted her to write a grant, bring his art show to the school, and even get him to speak at the opening. Soon after that, half the teachers in the school were doing activities in their classrooms related to his work and integrating it into their curricula.

As she pondered the budding conflicts in her school, Pam turned back to Martha's journal to reread the latest entry and wondered what clues it held for her.

Martha's Journal:

What a great day! All day the gym was full of kids playing the "Travel Europe" game. Each group represented a different country, each with its own computer, and the software worked terrifically. The tape on the floor designating each country's boundaries stayed put, and nobody tripped over the wiring. I couldn't believe how into it the kids were. It was so funny when Italy and Spain needed to get to Finland and couldn't pass through German customs.

A lot of credit has to go to Terri and Sam and how well they prepped the kids earlier in the week. It's really something when a whole group of us pull together, work on a unit like this, with everyone adding ideas, and then we actually do it. Then again, a lot of the credit goes to Pam. It's not every principal who would allow a third of her faculty to disrupt the gym, the library, and the lunch schedules for a few weeks. She not only allowed us, she encouraged us.

I remember when Pam came to Currier. Has it been six years already? We were all worried that she'd be a pushover because she didn't seem to have a strong set of plans for the school. Was she going to be the stooge for central office? Was the old guard going to manipulate her? She talked so much about wanting to listen to our ideas and parents' goals for their kids, we thought she might be one of these yes-to-everybody principals.

Well she sure turned out different, at least as I see it. If she hadn't encouraged me to get into the electronic media and library bit, I'd have gone crazy and probably would have left education altogether. I mean, she had a pretty clear idea that teachers need to be encouraged to lead, that we have the greatest knowledge of our kids and the creativity to teach them what they need. I remember when she said, "My job is to help you get focused on what the kids need, to support you, and then to get out of your way."

Pam has made my work as an educator truly rewarding. I'm now involved in a lot of classrooms and working with a lot of other teachers. The library media center is being used all the time. Currier has been recognized statewide for our use of technology in integrating themes across the curriculum.

The only reservation I have is that some teachers haven't gotten on board. I've done demonstrations in Sheila's room at least a dozen times, and I've talked to her till I'm blue in the face. She and several others still won't use the computers or the library except to send kids there for me to teach. Then there are the teachers who seem to get bent out of shape every time we have one of these interdisciplinary units, the way Bud just did when we wanted to use "his" gym. I couldn't believe that tirade about tape on "my floor." What's he in it for anyway? What makes him think it's *his* floor? If Pam hadn't stepped in and assured him about the tape and the wires and then come up with a place for him to hold his classes, I don't know what I would have said to him.

I have less and less patience with these teachers who haven't had a creative idea their entire lives. Not only do they force drudgery on their kids every single day—of course, calling it discipline and skill work—but they're becoming more and more obstructive to the rest of us and our efforts. This is getting to be a real problem.

Reading Martha's journal prompted Pam to turn to her keyboard and write the following entry:

> Boy, as I read this, I feel so conflicted. I don't want to squelch Martha's enthusiasm. She's exactly what I've always dreamt of having in a teacher. But I don't know if I can consistently keep her needs in synch with everyone else's. When Frank approached me today, he was being rather indirect, but I could tell that underneath he was boiling about not being able to move forward on his plan. In some ways I feel guilty that I have everyone energized and then see them thwarted in their efforts. Maybe I'd be better off backing away from such blanket encouragement.
>
> I remember when I first met Frank. He actually introduced me to Currier. He's just blossomed over the last few years. I remember when he announced that he had made it his goal to be the best second-grade teacher in the state.
>
> He has really worked to fulfill that goal. He has attended so many workshops on early childhood education. Now he's viewed as a regional resource on developmental learning. I'll never forget when he proposed setting up an early learner team (ELT), a group of five teachers teaching six- to nine-year-old children in nongraded classrooms. It's so admirable the way he has championed the inclusion of special needs students in regular classrooms, each at his or her own developmental level. Of course, the great thing is that this is the case for every class at Currier now.

Pam wondered if Frank's journal would shed light on the dynamics developing among her teachers. She flipped through her stack of journals, found Frank's, and read:

> Is it the weather? Or is it me? Or is it the school? I've been feeling really frustrated the last couple of weeks. And I'm picking it up from the rest of the early learner team too. Everybody seems sort of edgy.

I think part of it is the backlash we're getting from some parents. When Mrs. Corchiani and those other parents came in last week wanting to see proof that Kerry was doing as well in the ELT as third graders in traditional programs are doing, it did get a bit dicey. As the team leader, I felt personally responsible for handling the situation. Actually, I think Pam should have been there. I mean, she's the principal; she's supposed to handle these things. The rest of us are teachers. But there we were, facing the doubting Thomases ourselves. Truthfully, I couldn't even tell how the parents took what we said, but I do know it was upsetting for the team.

I think the other thing that's been bothering all of us is losing our time in the gym and the library. Those times have been so important to us and the kids. For the last three weeks, that middle-grade Europe game has been set up in the gym two days each week. We haven't been able to get our kids in there for their developmental games. Worse yet, we've had to do P.E. in our classrooms or the cafeteria. That really cuts into our faculty planning time, which is so important to our teaming. We've got the same problems when Martha closes the library because she's in the gym with that game.

I think we're starting to feel that the ELT is getting squeezed by the middle grades' integrated curriculum events. They really do take over the school, and all of us have to adjust to what they're doing. Peg is really getting bothered by it. She came right out at the last faculty meeting on Monday and said it: "Why should our kids suffer because you need to use this and that, have this and that room, and move our gym around the school?" It is making it more difficult to keep our program integrated.

Where's Pam on this? Peg thinks that Pam will say yes to anything Martha asks for, that Pam has a soft spot for the middle grades. I see how she could think that. But Pam has been terrifically supportive of the ELT and of me. When she first came here, I figured she was so green as a principal that she wouldn't be able to get anything going. But she went to bat with the superintendent and the board for developmental curriculum, then for full inclusion. When

Bill was over for dinner last Saturday, he mentioned how much he and the other board members respect Pam. Pam is great at getting things started, and she has stuck with teachers who want to take leadership roles as Martha and I have.

I'm just not sure she knows what to do now. She's still supportive of everyone. But now we have a situation where we're in each other's way, and it's starting to create hard feelings. Pam doesn't appear to know what to do with this any more than we do. Most of the time, she seems to gloss over it, or she says we need to work it out ourselves. Those meetings aren't getting us anywhere. We always end up with some kind of compromise that makes someone grumble. Lately, the grumbling seems to be more constant, and most of it's in our team.

How can we discuss this? Pam shows so much confidence in what we're doing, and we need her to be there for us in the future. I don't really think she'd be offended if we brought it up, but you never know. . . . There are so many things coming at principals, it's hard to figure out when to bring up something like this. Maybe it's best just to tough it out. Perhaps after the term ends in April will be a better time.

Pam continues in her journal to mull over the worrisome situation brewing among her staff:

When I started this job, I remember so clearly thinking I was going to be a savior to the teachers. Having been a somewhat rebellious teacher myself, I decided to go into administration primarily to provide teachers the opportunities to make happen what they believed in—quite unlike the environment in which I taught. Now I'm sitting here chuckling at my own arrogance, filled with countless questions about teacher leadership.

How can I assist both Martha and Frank in making their visions become reality without creating chaos in the school? What will I do when someone presents an idea that isn't in synch with my vision? Or what if an idea seems antithetical to the staff's collaborative vision? How can I be sure what the staff's vision is? It's clear that there were many things I hadn't thought through. I actually believed it was as simple as encouraging all the teachers to think about what they believed in, what they wanted to make happen for kids, and supporting them to "just do it." Right now, though, I'm wondering if I haven't opened a can of worms that I cannot control.

Principals today are encouraged to develop their teachers into "communities of leaders" (Barth, 1990). Yet, we all acknowledge that we are just beginning to understand this critical dimension of the job. Many principals feel the same tensions that Pam feels as she involves teachers in making decisions on a host of matters outside the traditional confines of their classrooms. The many ideas, beliefs, and practices of creative, caring teachers do not fit neatly into a single, coherent community.

How does a principal assist teachers like Martha and Frank to bring their own visions to reality without creating chaos in the school? What skills must principals utilize to facilitate teachers taking on leadership roles? How do they encourage teachers to be leaders yet respect one another and the unity of the school's mission? These are some of the questions that Pam's story suggests to us. Follow the conversation between Becky and Gordy as they offer their own perspectives on our list of questions.

Dear Becky:

I sympathize with Pam and the position she's gotten herself in. She's obviously well intentioned. She seems to be familiar with the literature on teacher empowerment and teacher leadership—I hear echoes of Maeroff (1988), Lieberman (1988), Rosenholtz (1989), and Bolman and Deal (1993). She's certainly walked her walk and talked her talk: these two groups of teachers are unleashed thoroughbreds indeed!

But I'm worried that Pam's not holding up her end of the deal. To her credit, she's very aware of the conflicts among her staff:

Martha and her colleagues have encroached on Bud and on the ELT; Peg's resentment is boiling over into the faculty meeting. Pam's relationships with her staff are so open that, luckily, she's hearing through these journals that some teachers—Frank and Peg specifically—are beginning to wonder about her leadership. The warning signals are flashing everywhere.

What might she do? How does she get all the worms back in the can? Can she even control the worms enough to get them back in? I think Pam needs to assert herself more—not to control everything, but to regulate the activities of these thoroughbreds to assure that the school remains a healthy place for everyone. She seems to have abdicated her responsibility to hold the school together—either because she's so gung-ho for teacher empowerment or because she lacks the skills, time, and energy to keep everyone pulling together as a whole, not just individually or in teams. Her rather Pollyanna-ish belief in unleashing the creative power of all her staff has led some of them—Peg, Frank and the ELT, and probably Bud too—to have serious doubts about her leadership.

Pam's got to set clearer guidelines for the way teachers and teams work within the school. She needs to start by changing her own mind-set about her teachers. She says she believes her role is "to help others sort out their visions and to help them realize these visions." That sounds good until one person or team's beliefs about what should happen—like those of Martha, Sam, and Terri—make it impossible for the beliefs of others to happen. Pam has to stop thinking of her staff as thoroughbreds that run individually in a race and to start thinking about them as draft horses that pull together in a race. Most important, Pam has to see herself as the harness and the driver for this team.

Pam needs to be realistic and to look at whether teachers in a busy school actually can coordinate their efforts with one another. Realistically, I don't think they can. They're too busy with kids and teaching. They've been encouraged to develop individual visions, not a collective one. Anyway, some probably don't have the interpersonal skills to work out differences with one another.

Frank hit the nail on the head in his journal: "Where is Pam on this?" Where is she when Frank and his team need her to help resolve differences with a parent or, more important, with Martha and her group? To save her credibility as a leader, Pam needs to assert guidelines for teams and individual teachers to follow when what they want to do with their kids will encroach on others' plans. She can't just leave it to them "to work it out ourselves," as Frank said. The fact is, they haven't been able to work it out. Now staff are seeing her as someone who, as Frank puts it, "is great at getting things started" but not so good at helping them mature.

Pam needs to do two things immediately to create the harness that will permit everyone to pull together instead of working at cross-purposes. She needs to clarify the mission and the vision of the school. It sounds as if individual and team visions may be diverging from one another. The central values of the school must be clear so that Pam and the staff can look to these school goals for guidance when two of their individual or team programs conflict. For example, when Martha used the gym, abrogating Bud and the entire school's rights to use it, she and her colleagues were asserting that their programs had precedence over the regular uses of the gym. But it doesn't sound as though everyone understood or agreed to that. Pam's job is to adjudicate those decisions before such incidents happen and to assure everyone that the whole school's mission is served by such practices.

The other thing Pam needs to do is to be much more active in working among all her teachers and teams. The journals help her stay plugged into what they're doing and how they're feeling, but it sounds as though she needs to intervene more often. I think this will require her to identify boundaries more frequently between individuals and groups and to define when they're straying from the school's mission or into somebody else's territory. She may not like this much because she will find herself drawing limits around the Marthas on her staff. Martha, who wrote that Pam has "made my work as an educator truly rewarding" by liberating her to follow her own vision, may not feel so liberated. But Pam is losing credibility and trust with Peg, who believes that Pam will "say yes to anything Martha asks for." Pam's got to assert some rules for working out interteam differences, and she's got to be a fair, even-handed arbitrator among her staff, or she's going to find herself in the middle of a real civil war!

I'm looking forward to hearing your viewpoint, Becky.

> Sincerely,
> Gordy

Dear Gordy,

You're tough! Poor Pam. You're putting all of the responsibility for her staff working together on her shoulders. I'm not so sure I agree. You talk about her holding up her end of the deal? What about the staff? Is she totally responsible for resolving conflicts among staff members?

I do agree with your suggestion about clarifying the mission and vision of the school. I'd suggest she read some of the literature on the articulating of core values (Saphier and D'Auria, 1993; Glickman, 1985; Fullan, 1993) to help her decide how to do this. I suspect that, in keeping with her beliefs, she would engage the whole staff in the process. Though the process would be lengthy, it would be time well spent. They'd likely develop some of the skills they're lacking in terms of dealing with one another.

Much of the literature suggests that the principal or a consultant could facilitate the process. In this case, I think it would be important to have an outside facilitator. This way, Pam would be part of the group and able to share her beliefs. She also may want to ask the facilitator to spend time individually with her to sort out her relationship with the staff. This whole business of shared leadership is still so murky that the answers often can't be found in the literature. Personally, I've learned the most from discussions with those who understand group dynamics (Kallick, 1989).

There's nothing like an outside eye to provide perspective on a group interaction.

If I were Pam, I'd look for a facilitator trained in teaching conflict-resolution skills. You mentioned that Pam may not have the skills to keep everyone pulling together as a team. I wonder if the staff has them. None of us needs to be defensive about this because we haven't been trained in the skills necessary for sharing leadership. Probably the least discussed skills in education schools are those relating to conflict resolution. Pam's responsibility is to set a tone in which conflict is viewed as fruitful to the growth of the school. She also needs to set the expectation that the staff develop the skills to work through any conflict. There are many facilitators, workshops, and literature available to help her (Senge, 1994).

After everyone has begun to develop some conflict-resolution skills, I'd be inclined to set up a formal structure to which the staff can bring conflicts such as Peg and Frank's. This sends the message that it is natural to have conflicts. They're part of collaborating and unleashing energies, and it is important to address them. My guess is that eventually the staff will work through these conflicts on their own without using a formal structure.

You indicated that Pam's own beliefs and needs are tied to her difficulties. I agree, but I think all leaders, to some degree, get their own needs met through their interaction with staff. To varying degrees, we all want to be liked; we all want to make sure every-thing goes right, and we all want to see our visions come to fruition. It would be dishonest not to acknowledge that a leader has needs and is probably consciously or unconsciously motivated by these needs. In fact, I believe we need to give leaders permis-sion to do so.

I would go a step further and say that it is really important for a leader to recognize his or her needs and to be aware of how the leadership role is fulfilling them. Then the question can be asked: are the fulfillment of my needs and those of staff, students, and school community complementary to one another? We need to challenge ourselves as leaders to understand our needs, to know when they're being met, and to discern when that is productive for others—not an easy task.

Sincerely,
Becky

As Pam's story illustrates, for principals the efforts of many well-intentioned teachers short-circuit because their autonomous efforts are at odds with the collective efforts of the school community. Many principals who choose to foster teacher leadership claim that they feel incapable of handling this tension well. This feeling has its roots in an unclear image of teacher development and an uncertainty about how to foster it, given the demands of the job (Leithwood, 1990). Traditionally, teachers have been perceived as reluctant to think of themselves as leaders (Troen and Boles, 1994). In this concluding section, we acknowledge the complexity of this task and the courage it takes for all members of a school to make sense of the tensions between teacher autonomy and the greater sense of community.

We base our thinking on our own experiences, which have shown that collaboration is a process that can be learned. We believe that it is important for principals and teachers themselves to learn to collaborate in order to create shared leadership in their schools. The actions of one individual alone—principal or teacher—cannot determine the leadership model for a school (Rost, 1991). Many teachers and principals have discovered that this shared leadership occurs only when they are brought into genuine relationship with one another.

The focus among teachers and principals is usually on goals and objectives that culminate in measurable outcomes. We believe that principals and teachers should make learning how to collaborate a fundamental goal in and of itself. As both Becky and Gordy suggest in Pam's case, the essential and vital groundwork for principals and teachers lies in working with one another to clarify mutual purposes. This process, in our view, involves deliberately creating the conditions necessary for good conversation and listening. This can be accomplished by nurturing the many ingredients that enhance collaboration, such as investing trust, reaching agreement or accepting disagreement, displaying care, giving affirmation, sharing feelings, and expressing empathy.

Collaboration is more organic than mechanical. Every group of adults and children has its own character and culture. Sometimes it is the synergy of different people and diverse points of view that yields the new or unexpected result that defines good collaborative effort. While we offer no simple formulas for translating these forms into action, three questions are central to any school effort at establishing collaboration: what is the process unique to our community that will make it advantageous for us to work together? How can we ensure a way for everyone to have a key role in the work? Finally, whose interests ultimately will be served by what we are doing together?

The hardest and perhaps the most important element of collaboration for principals and teachers is the commitment to do it at all and to take the work seriously. This commitment requires that teachers and principals together address these three questions. As they pursue their collective response to each question, they will explore both the potential benefits of collaboration and their collective will to invest in it.

We believe that adults in schools can learn to collaborate more effectively and humanely with each other, but principals cannot do it without teachers and vice versa. As obvious as this may seem, recall Pam's case. All too often the responsibility for collaboration is left solely to the principal. We believe that principals and teachers must together set the conditions for shared leadership and decision making. To embark on this path, principals and teachers risk working themselves out of their traditional roles. A paradoxical component for principals is knowing when to get out of the way and at the same time keep the work going. Principals must be sensitive to the subtle shifts in power that develop as they encourage shared leadership—especially the shifts in their own roles as principals. Similarly, teachers must be sensitive and alert to these conditions.

Principals and teachers frequently make assumptions about each other's intentions with respect to sharing leadership, but rarely do they deal with these assumptions in a structured way. We believe that adults in schools benefit from learning how to test their inferences rather than accepting them as truths. We acknowledge how truly difficult it is to engage in open, honest dialogue of this kind. Yet, learning to collaborate is predicated fundamentally on our abilities to voice how we're making sense of things and to share our collective *sense* of the truth as opposed to the truth.

Thus, the kind of collaboration we envision assumes that principals and teachers can make sense of the challenges they face, not only through ideas but also through feelings and the meanings they attach to them. We assume that development, creativity, and growth occur through new ways of interpreting personal and interpersonal events. Finally, and most important, it is often the conflicts, the uncertainties, the doubt, and ambivalence that offer genuine openings and opportunities for new learning.

We believe that as principals and teachers find ways to work with one another along these lines, some of the traditional hurdles to effective problem solving will start to disappear. As staff begin to share more openly their collective responsibility for designing responses to the various educational problems they face, they will strengthen their relationship with one another. And as their sense of being a team grows, they will be more capable of addressing the issues and problems particular to teaching and learning.

Respecting teacher autonomy and working toward a sense of community requires good will, new skills and knowledge, and the leadership of everyone involved. Principals who encourage teachers to play a larger leadership role are willing and able to look at the nature of their own influence differently. Likewise, teachers who seek to lead must learn to view their influence in a different light. Leadership, viewed in this way, is ultimately a kind of community sense making. At its core, it reflects the ways in which a group of people relate to one another and how they consciously become a unified, closely integrated group that is more than the sum of its parts.

Chapter Nine

Trusting in Community

Thinking back over our seven persisting questions, we suspect that you have had a variety of thoughts and feelings about being a principal. These questions may seem to be all over the map, stretching from issues of discipline and justice to the fundamental purposes of schools to issues of ownership and control. You may wonder: how does any one person keep all this straight? How can I have answers to all of these questions?

We would like to share with you two fundamental values that have helped us make the most of the tensions of school leadership. They have anchored our thoughts, feelings, and actions in our work *as* principals and *with* principals. The first of these is trust in community; the second, trust in yourself as a leader. We have found that these principles join as yin and yang to shape the principal's success at making productive partners of the forces behind the seven persisting questions. We hope you will find in this chapter some new approaches to understanding how your leadership is integral to a community of learning, caring people. As this deeper understanding grows, you will all gain trust in the school as a community. In Chapter Ten, we explore how this trust nurtures trust in yourself as a leader.

The seven persisting questions we have explored germinate from diverse and often competing forces in schools. A student's individual needs conflict with the school's need for consistency and rules, as in the case of Gerry Taylor and Sandy. Parents' desires clash with teachers' desires, as in the case of Sherrie and Mr. and Mrs. Wright. Sometimes it is a teacher's or a teacher group's conviction that runs counter to another teacher group's conviction, as in Pam's case. And sometimes a teacher's interest runs up against the principal's judgment, as in the case of Carl, Melissa, and the nonparticipators.

The essence of these tensions, of course, lies in the uncomfortable coexistence of differing philosophies, values, interests, and personalities. Schools in the United States—especially public schools—serve diverse people with diverse aspirations, backgrounds, and educational capacities. When we try to serve them all equally well, the inherent differences among them often translate into competition among them: for special attention, for top priority, for resources, or simply because one group needs to feel "We're right and you're not." The principal, by virtue of his or her formal role, lives constantly in the bubbling cauldron of these mixed and often competing interests and needs.

We believe that schools thrive when they honor these differences. Schools where people learn from one another's differences rather than compete with or suppress one another are schools that foster trust, open inquiry, and democratic ideals. In the preceding seven chapters, each principal's story might have been *solved* by the principal imposing a decision, siding with one side, or orchestrating a behind-the-scenes conclusion.

Our approach is the mirror opposite of this. We have seen that when the principal trusts in community and turns over the responsibility for a collaborative solution to the competing parties, both staff and students reap powerful benefits. When the people of a school become productive partners, they can make use of their own differences. In such schools, tensions become sources of creation.

Four Basic Values that Support This View

Modeling Democracy

Schools in this country were founded on the premise that an educated populace is essential to a successful democracy. This has not changed; we still need to prepare students to be effective citizens with the skills of critical thinking, an ability to see one another's perspectives, an understanding of how to be part of a political process, and a sense of responsibility for the collective.

As many have argued since John Dewey's day, children cannot learn these values in institutions that do not live by them (Gutmann, 1987; Apple, 1990). When the adults who inhabit a school function as a democratic community, resolving inevitable differences and making complex decisions in an open, participatory, and respectful manner, students will learn these ways as well. This necessitates building a community that encompasses all the rights and responsibilities found in a democratic society and applies them to each individual. Schools need to model democracy for their children and citizens.

Creating a Whole that Is Greater than the Sum of Its Parts

The more we observe community within schools, the more we are convinced that a staff that functions as a community offers far greater opportunities for student and staff growth than they can as a collection of individuals. A synergy is generated when the institution's challenges are laid before the group, and the group openly struggles to create new practices that all members can support and implement (Fullan and Hargreaves, 1991; Senge, 1990a). Not only is the challenge met, but the isolation that educators so often experience becomes a thing of the past. When an all-school project takes place, when teachers join to share materials and ideas, or when a grade level decides to work together for a two-day block, the impact of the effort always is greater than the sum of the individual efforts.

Nurturing Healthier Relationships for Staff and Students

The isolation that currently exists in many schools is an unhappy and unhealthy state. We hear stories repeatedly concerning teachers who arrive in the morning, go to their classrooms, and manage to go unseen until the end of the day when they return to their cars. They have very little, if any, adult contact, receive no support, and have no one with whom to share either the joys or the difficulties of teaching. Where else do we expect twenty-five human beings to perform complex and valuable work with so little interpersonal adult contact?

Conversely, what happens when we trust in the community to care for its members? We observe doors opening, students moving flexibly throughout the building, and relationships growing among students and teachers (Johnson, 1990; Barth, 1990). We also observe people laughing more, reaching out both to give and to receive support, and building a camaraderie that goes beyond school. We see too increased comfort with differences of opinion and practice, energetic conversation about new practice, and fulfillment derived from jobs that have greater meaning (Little, 1993).

Meeting the Leader's Needs

We do not often acknowledge that leaders of schools have needs. Principals work hard to meet staff, student, and parental needs. But principals are people too! They lose neither the need for close relationships nor the desire to be part of a collegial team when they take the job of principal.

Building community has a partially selfish dimension in that it provides us with a sense of broad-based support for decisions. It also provides a setting conducive to developing warm relationships among staff and helps principles overcome the feeling that they are "alone at the top" (Sergiovanni, 1992; Donaldson, 1991).

The Principal as Creator and Sustainer of Community

We contend that the many tensions that surface in the principal's work in a school day are more creatively and effectively resolved when adults work together as a healthy community. In fact, in a shared leadership environment, many of these situations never really surface for the principal at all.

How can the principal create and sustain community? The straightforward answer is that alone, he or she cannot. True communities are not created by a single person. However, the principal is in a position to influence powerfully how adults identify and resolve important dilemmas in their work and with one another. This *shaping influence* is an essential leadership function of the principal (Sergiovanni, 1992; Cunningham and Gresso, 1993; Wheatley, 1992). If the school is beset by differences of opinion, belief, or practice, the very essence of the school as a learning community can be threatened by the ways people act with one another. The school as a social unit—parents, children, and staff—either thrives or withers, depending on how the differences are resolved. We think of it much as we think of exercising muscles: we all use muscles everyday; whether we pull or tear a muscle or we strengthen it to use another day hinges on *how* we approach and carry through our exercise.

Principals benefit from understanding how to include all legitimate interests and all interested people in open debate and mutually supportive solution finding. We believe this must begin with thoughtful consideration of the principles and values that underlie democratic life. A leader cannot cultivate community if he or she doesn't believe in it or trust in its value.

An important discovery for us in this process of reflection has been acknowledging that there is no one best system in education (Tyack, 1974). The more we study learning and teaching styles, the more we see diversity in American society and culture, and the more we recognize how bewildering the problems facing our schools are, the more confident we become that sharing responsibility for teaching children is the only sensible strategy. To do this, we must understand the many values and philosophies within our schools and be versatile at forging the interpersonal and philosophical links that will permit all adults to serve our children the best way they can. This, in turn, requires us to know ourselves, our values, and our effects on others.

We suggest that principals lead their schools in the process of community building by first asking questions. How will we work together to foster a culture supportive of every school member's learning? Can we acknowledge the essential value of each individual, which is necessary for effective learning, while respecting the divergent goals and styles of each? How do we guide the process to develop in our students the cooperative life habits that their futures will demand? Then the principal facilitates a process through which adults can create their own answers and design actions to match. To accomplish this, principals need the skills to facilitate group discussion, to sustain the group's efforts through times of conflict and ambiguity, and to keep the group's attention steadfastly fixed on the benefits that will accrue to students.

As adults become collectively able to respond to the complex challenges highlighted by our seven questions, they will find themselves balancing some seeming opposites. We have identified some of these and invite you to consider others that pertain to your situation.

Lay Wisdom and Professional Expertise

Sherrie's story and, to some extent, Bob McCormick's resources dilemma highlight a constant tension arising from the differences in educators' knowledge and perspectives and parent and community members' knowledge and perspectives. Clearly, if a sense of community is to develop, lay wisdom and professional expertise not only must be valued but also must be merged. Parents and teachers, administrators, and counselors bring unique perspectives on each child to the table. If they are all to collaborate, as they must, on a single strategy for that child's growth and learning, they must understand and appreciate the uniqueness of one another. The same can be said for differences between educators, citizens, and policy makers, whose primary obligation is to the municipality and its voters.

The roles of these groups used to be much clearer than they are now. Parents have entered "professional territory" through their own efforts and through educators' willingness to include them in curricular and management issues. Greater political activity among citizens and educators alike has generated opinions and initiatives on testing, setting standards, capping spending, assuring the rights of minorities, and a host of other issues that profoundly affect schools.

These developments call upon community builders to understand an expanding directory of people, groups, and points of view. In this vein, principals find themselves facilitating meetings where participants may neither understand nor value one another. Principals need to be comfortable with and capable of negotiating understanding and mediating action among these interests in a win-win fashion. Working within the tension that exists between lay and professional perspectives requires principals to model democratic values and processes in their face-to-face and day-to-day work.

Expediency and Participation

Another tension that arises in the journey toward community results from, on the one hand, the need to accomplish certain tasks and, on the other, the need to have everyone involved in decisions that are of mutual importance. All three of us entered the principalship believing that everyone should be involved in decisions that will affect them. It wasn't long before we realized there are times when this is impossible.

Emergencies arose in which decisions had to be made immediately. Or time simply ran out, as it did on Gerry as she deliberated over Sandy. Sometimes, no matter how much participation we had, we could not obtain consensus. In those cases, it was necessary to make a decision to move forward, as was the case for Sue Ann and for Herbert Day. At other times, everyone couldn't be physically involved in the process, so the principal, as in the case of

Bob McCormick, ended up running messages back and forth among competing groups. Much to our surprise, not all staff wanted to be involved in most decisions. More than once, we were told, "What are administrators paid for anyway? We just want to be left alone to teach."

One of the principal's major challenges is discerning the extent to which broad participation in discussions and decisions is warranted, sensible, possible, and necessary. This decision is not his or hers alone to make. With respect to many issues, other people already have established a stake and an opinion; the principal's task is to facilitate their involvement. For other issues, the principal must seek out staff and citizens with the expertise, the judgment, or the appropriate authority to arrive at the best recommendation or decision. In nearly all cases, the principal must consider children, staff, and parents who may be affected, and they must facilitate appropriate degrees of involvement for each.

This is no mean feat and, like many of the tasks we've discussed, it is never finished. In each of our chapter conversations, the principal faced a challenge by giving over responsibility to others and then orchestrating their working together. Strong communities are characterized by members who feel responsible for the quality of life and work in the community. They want to have a hand in affairs. When they do, their ideas and energies enrich the experience of everyone. But the principal in a community of learners is often saddled with the job of seeing that all this involvement goes smoothly. It costs time, energy, and often money. Principals often need to help others with communication issues, decision-making processes, and issues of role boundaries.

Collective and Individual
Ownership and Responsibility

Inevitably, staff members run the full gamut between those who give themselves totally to the school as a whole and those who believe their jobs are to work in their classrooms. Carl faced such a dilemma with Melissa. So did Sue Ann Podolski and Herbert Day. A premise of community building is that each member of the school share some degree of ownership and responsibility for the health and welfare of the entire school. How does the principal respond to staff members—or parents and citizens, for that matter—who do not believe in or do not understand such whole school responsibility?

As we noted earlier, building community has important student and staff benefits. The pooling and coordination of ideas, techniques, resources, and strategies create a synergy best described in the adage, "It takes a whole village to raise a child." Yet some adults are lone eagles. Their talents are individual talents, and their work style is independent. Others, like the nonparticipators in Carl's school, may have philosophical or personal reasons for not joining the principal's or school community's mission. Still others, like the two teams in Pam's school, are so intent upon the conflict with one another that bringing them on board seems nearly futile.

As you think about these cases again, consider the skills and talents needed to draw from every adult a minimum of collective responsibility and ownership. To accomplish this, it is helpful to have people, perhaps including you, who can lead a process that gives all people an authentic voice. Coalition-building skills and persuasion are also useful. Perhaps most important is personal trustworthiness: if the principal's intentions are clear and altruistic, and he or she has been proven worthy of personal trust, members of the community will respond by placing trust in the mission the principal seeks to fulfill (Bennis and Nanus, 1985). For some, only then will it be safe to venture beyond their own classrooms, their departmental "fiefdoms," or their homes to share in the community's voyage toward greater learning and belonging for all.

My Authority and Consensus Authority

Intertwined with all of these tensions is a more personal one. Trusting in the community's judgments and actions requires the principal to rein in and sometimes even to abdicate authority and power traditionally assigned to him or her. Students, teachers, secretaries, janitors, and parents generally ascribe to the principal instant authority, responsibility, and specialized expertise. School boards, superintendents, and civic and business leaders usually assume that principals operate unilaterally and decisively and that they have the power to implement their decisions. It is not uncommon for educators to seek the principalship with these notions of independent, singular authority in mind.

Many principals quickly recognize the trade-offs inherent in this presumption of authority. The breadth and frequency of problems to solve and the variety of people to deal with often outstrip the principal's knowledge, control, personal influence, and energy. To maintain authority, principals frequently create systems to narrow the business of school, so they can control decisions and actions within this more manageable band. Soon, however, principals discover that the educational business of the school requires widespread participation and decision making that is close to the classroom and the child. Gerry Taylor discovered this when she was forced to make a decision about Sandy without sufficient information to make it a good decision. Similarly, Herbert Day was caught between top-down expectations to create a house system and the realities of teachers who did not see the value in it.

Many principals understand the vast potential of community building for developing *consensus authority* around beliefs and practices. Research on school improvement and change (Fullan, 1993) reinforces this understanding and encourages principals to forgo traditional hierarchical definitions of power, authority, and responsibility and, instead, to generate collective definitions. This is very complicated work, as the seven principals in our stories demonstrate. In every school are teachers, staff, and parents who want principals to shoulder the lion's share of the authority. Most school districts and most state laws require principals to make employment and personnel judgments and decisions. School boards delegate authority in specific ways to superintendents and principals, assigning to them special responsibilities over teachers, students, and even parents.

Most principals feel caught between a "top" that makes demands and a "bottom" that does not comply easily with their demands. These principals come to feel the typical isolation of the middle manager. Principals are neither fish nor fowl, so to speak, neither exclusively members of central management nor of the teacherhood. For them, the basic socioemotional needs for affiliation, for workplace friendships, for being oneself at work come into conflict with the realities of the position. New principals say they feel people in the school drawing away from them. They feel that people are watching how they wield their authority. They wonder how they can be colleagues and friends while also being in charge. This is the essence of Pam's dilemma with the conflicting teacher groups in her school, of Bob McCormick's budget conflict with his seventh-grade team and his superintendent, and of Carl's supervisory quandary about Melissa.

No matter how hard they try, principals never really shake this authority tension because the principal is the point around which these issues focus. Many people believe that principals are doing their job correctly if they do not consult on decisions but rather lay down the law. Others think that principals are fulfilling job expectations if they do just the opposite: empower others to make their own decisions. Still others believe that principals need a strong public persona, so strong that they can command the authority and the freedom to shape the schools to their own personal vision.

In the final analysis, few principals escape the presumption of power and the vast array of emotions it provokes among constituents. Inevitably, principals question their own beliefs about the legitimacy of their authority. How do I know I will make the right decision just because they expect me to? What gives me the expertise to know what should happen next? Yesterday I was teaching seventh-grade math, and today they expect me to know about boilers, bus routes, and home economics. Such questions permeate the life of principals and add to the sense of being alone.

We believe that the burden of this mantle of authority must be shared if a school is to thrive. Furthermore, we believe that this mantle must be shared if the *principal* is to thrive. The number, variety, and frequency of problems hurtling at caring principals are simply too great for any one person to handle. To attempt to resist them alone destines a principal to burnout. Consider that our seven principals were each dealing with a single problem. Then consider a scenario in which each of them is dealing with all seven problems at once. The second is by far the more common scenario for many principals!

As principals, your challenge is to trust in the school community's collective judgment and authority to resolve its own questions and problems. This will help the school community to exercise its authority responsibly. You might begin by engaging others in deciding which issues are best handled unilaterally, which by committees, and which by the whole community. When do matters so affect all members of the community that all must be a part of their resolution? The way you engage others in answering these questions will determine the extent of people's trust in the school and in the you.

You engender trust by helping others to discuss and decide who should have responsibility and authority in matters pertaining to children and programs. Then it is up to you to facilitate the development of collective action strategies. You need not exercise authority unilaterally or feel that you alone are responsible for everything in the school. You can effectively negotiate this authority question with people, including your superiors, who want you to have sole control and authority.

We have in this chapter suggested that you wrestle with the seven persisting questions and consider sharing the burden with fellow members of your school community. We caution against believing in (and thus relying upon) the superiority of expert knowledge, the benefits of expediency, the merits of individual ownership and accountability, or the necessity to exercise singular authority. Indeed, each of these is necessary to a degree. But as the primary tenets of your principalship, these beliefs and approaches do not lead to community. Rather, they lead to an environment where people with real interests in children are excluded from fulfilling their responsibilities, where thoughtful deliberation and collective action are cut short, and where trust in one another's information, resources, and judgment cannot grow. This kind of school, as Johnson (1990), Fullan and Hargreaves (1991), and Sizer (1984) have argued, is not a school where children and adults learn.

We think that the school community's ability to trust in itself to deliver what children need hinges on your trust in the community. As you ponder your own work as or with a principal, you might ask, When I (or a principal I know) come face-to-face with a challenge, do I shoulder the responsibility for it, or do I view it as *our* challenge? We contend that if you do the latter, the people you work with will come to see major challenges as theirs. Your faith in them and your commitment to community problem solving and action will nurture their faith in themselves and in the school. Schools with such communities of interest flourishing within them can take on any challenge, any persisting question, and can develop from it constructive actions and mutual support to carry those actions into practice.

Chapter Ten

Trusting in Yourself

Throughout our book, we have returned again and again to the persistent urge we felt as principals to solve people's problems and to bring order to their existence at school. The seven tensions that recur in principals' work can feel like centrifugal forces spinning people, programs, the building, and tempers *away* from the core mission. As principals, we felt an obligation to balance these forces with a strong gravitational pull back toward order and the common mission. We suspect you have experienced this urge to hold your school's world together as well.

We caution you, however, to resist this urge—at least to resist believing it is your solitary responsibility to make life within your school coherent for everyone. Our discussions of the seven tensions describe not only how impossible this task is for one person but also how the principal's need to control can damage the educational lifeblood of a school (McNeil, 1986). Yet, you might say, everybody looks to the principal to provide a foundation of stability for the school; everyone wants the principal to be wise, self-assured, confident, available, boundlessly energetic, just, sympathetic, tough when necessary, and much more! How am I to do this, you might wonder, if not by imposing order and control on the hubbub of my busy school?

In Chapter Nine, we urged you to consider trusting in community as an essential first step in developing a form of leadership that is collaborative rather than controlling. In this chapter, we suggest that trusting in yourself plays a central role in shaping your ability to trust in community.

Against the backdrop of tensions and questions that surround principals' work, your own confidence and dependability are tied to a fundamental faith that your influence over the school is healthful for all. Indeed, in our own experiences, we found that we could never anticipate or prepare ourselves and others for everything that came our way. Neither could we have the perfect—or even a good—answer for every problem. Instead, we had to trust that our talents, our good intentions, and our faith in others would help us lead our schools in ways that would benefit children.

We encourage you to reflect on the qualities within you that enable you to trust yourself as an educator and as a person. This trust in yourself as a leader cannot be blind; it must be affirmed by evidence that your leadership benefits the school. Regular reflection on your leadership activities and their effects on others gives you a steady diet of such evidence (Schön, 1983). If you are like us, this reflection not only will bring you face-to-face with doubts but also will help you recognize and affirm your talents and capacities.

Indeed, this self-reflection lies at the very heart of our making sense of ourselves as leaders (Jentz and Wofford, 1979). To the extent that we have felt out of touch with ourselves and with those we affected and were affected by, we have felt less able to trust that our leadership was healthful. Perhaps the deepest obligation a leader has is to engage continually in this reflective process of making sense of his or her effects on others and on the school. We share here five ideas that have helped us trust in ourselves as leaders (see Appendix B for a framework useful for self-reflection).

Be a Public Learner

Nothing erodes your trust in yourself more than feeling as if you are in a constant state of failure. Principals who conceive their central mission as having answers to all problems and issues that arise place themselves in this precarious position. We suggest that you consider your core activity to be learning, not giving answers. Trusting in yourself to learn is vastly more possible and rewarding than trusting yourself to have all the answers to everyone's problems.

The tensions we have described arise repeatedly in schools because the people who work in them and the people who entrust their children and tax dollars to them care profoundly about what goes on in them. Each person wants the school to succeed in his or her own way, but one institution cannot satisfy this rich array of needs and desires all at once. As principal, your challenge is not to satisfy them yourself but to enlist these people to become your partners in problem solving. We believe that for you to succeed, you must model effective problem finding, information sharing, and solution identifying—that is, you must be the lead learner in your school (Barth, 1990). We see leadership as a quest for increasingly effective learning and growth for everyone in the school, including the principal.

If you feel you have the freedom to fail and the support to learn from those failures and if you can give those gifts to your colleagues and students, won't you be contributing directly to the school's central mission? We urge you to think of yourself as part of a collective search for the best educational "next steps" for the children and adults in your school. The principals you have met in this book—including the three of us—are school leaders engaged in this process of learning. You too are the lead sense maker, among many other sense makers, in your school. You help everyone to ponder each challenge in light of your collective ideals and to find ways to shape the realities of your school to reach to those ideals. Your leadership activities can be understood to reflect a four-step process:

1. Evaluate in each situation the ideals that are competing with one another as people seek to move the school beyond its current realities.

2. Assess the capacities of the school to meet these ideals.

3. Identify what you and other members of the community can do to help unleash these capacities to meet these ideals.

4. Take action.

Thinking of this process as the core of your work will help you to stay focused on learning rather than on answer giving. Your learning will help you and everyone else evaluate important opportunities for growth in the questions that arise and to identify resources and steps for action within them. We think that if you engage in such learning publicly, your success as a principal will grow. We think also that your trust in yourself as a leader will grow.

Be a Linker of Resources

Just as you cannot have all the answers to the school's problems, neither can you be centrally involved in implementing every solution or good practice. You simply haven't enough hands, time, energy, or other personal resources. If you expect yourself to be the central cog in every major wheel at school, you will eventually erode your faith in yourself and others and your trust in your leadership.

Be a "linker" of resources to the people, problems, and opportunities that call for them. Schools have two enormous reservoirs of resources: existing technical knowledge and practices and existing human resources. Your challenge is to develop your own capacities to engage these technical and human resources, so they will productively meet the needs that arise as children pursue their learning. These linking capacities lie at the very core of your daily work. Understanding needs and knowing what resources the school has to meet these needs makes you a catalyst for problem solving more than a problem solver.

This linking function can be the backbone of your leadership. Its vertebrae consist of your collaborative relationships with professional and lay colleagues. Collaborative leadership rests on the assumption that no single leader can do it all. Quite to the contrary, this view assumes that, to be truly effective for all children, schools need many leaders. Each brings a unique blending of knowledge, talents, and energies to the collective task of making the school its best.

Your trust in yourself as a leader lies not in your success at directing and monitoring your colleagues but in your skill at creating the collaborative blend among them that will link them together in problem solving. You need not have vast technical knowledge to do this. Rather, you need to develop your interpersonal sensitivities and your abilities to include every responsible person in the ongoing conversation about the school's performance. You need to identify those human and technical resources that will move you forward as a school.

Be Clear About Core Values

You will feel buffeted by the forces that create all the recurring tensions. As you work to make sense of them, you will undoubtedly recognize the merits of different points of view and will wish to acknowledge the various convictions of the people who hold them. This is tough work. People will want you to side with them. Solutions will be presented to you as either-or choices. Political forces will line up on both sides. You will have every reason to question yourself and your ability to steer your school through such difficult choices. Your trust in yourself as a leader will, if your experience is like ours, be shaken.

Where can you turn for guidance and a sense of constancy? Undoubtedly, every principal has his or her own personal keel, whether it be people, religion, philosophy, or some other ultimate sense maker. We have found the need for a professional keel as well. In a democracy, leaders cannot impose their personal beliefs on their schools. Instead, our actions and thoughts need a core of principles clearly founded on values that support educational success for our children. As you operate on these values and share them publicly, you not only will articulate the professional mission of your leadership, but you will behave in a way that others can trust as well—even if they do not agree.

We have articulated our joint core values as we have developed this book. You will note that they are reflective of the seven persisting questions at the center of the principal's work:

1. *Justice:* All school members treat all children justly in the creation of a just community.

2. *Teaching:* All teachers and staff are valued and provide healthy, educative influences on all children.

3. *Purpose:* All children learn useful knowledge and skills and become healthy individuals and responsible members of society.

4. *Resources:* This school meets the needs of students within the real limits of public and personal resources.

5. *Change:* All teachers and staff seek constantly to improve in an atmosphere of respect.

6. *Ownership:* All school members respect each person's individuality, needs, and judgment in the service of unified goals that will benefit all children.

7. *Autonomy:* All school members respect the rights and responsibilities of parents, community, staff, and students to shape a collective direction and nature of education.

Your trust in yourself as a leader is rooted in knowing what is important to you—in having clarity about such core values as these. We believe that our core values reflect the heart of what democratic education means in our country (Gutmann, 1987; Tyack and Hansot, 1990; Cremin, 1961). You may approach school leadership from a different slant, or you may understand these same values in different terms. Our point is that your awareness of your core professional values, whatever they are, is necessary to your trusting in yourself as a leader. They help you to think and to act consistently with ideals that you believe are educationally and ethically sound. They give you and others a sense of your dependability and your trustworthiness.

Listen to Your School

Listening lies at the heart of being a learner and a linker. We mean listening in the broadest sense: staying attuned to the signals from children, parents, custodians, teachers, the building itself, and other sources that alert you to the state of the school and life within it. Traditional views of leadership resound not with listening but with "telling": the principal is typically portrayed as using his or her expertise and privileged knowledge to direct others on the right course. Telling, as our letters to one another illustrate, leads principals to presume that they know what is best for others. Such a presumption undermines the self-respect and responsibility of those who need these qualities the most if education is to succeed: teachers, students, and parents.

Listening to your school helps you succeed in two basic ways: it tells you where and how your leadership is most needed, and it tells you how you are doing as a leader. Think of the school as your teacher. Its people and patterns of daily activity can teach you where people are succeeding and where they are struggling, what issues are dominating peoples' attention, and where your focus needs to be directed. The school can also tell you who and where the resources are that you can call upon. Instead of having to conjure up appropriate solutions to problems from your own knowledge or from books and journals, you can listen to your school and discover solutions right under your nose.

Equally important, your school—and particularly your colleagues—can help you understand yourself as a leader. In our experience, it is extraordinarily difficult to get honest and accurate feedback on leadership effectiveness. We generally know what we are *trying* to do, and we have *feelings* about how effective we are, but we do not really know how effective we are in the eyes of those we hope to lead.

The three of us have benefited enormously from authentic feedback from trustworthy friends and colleague-critics. Together with our own reflections, this feedback has enabled us to determine more confidently what actions and approaches we should continue and what areas we should work hard to change. Without benefit of both this greater knowledge of our work and the confidence it brings, we would find it exceedingly difficult to trust that our leadership is effective.

Listen to Yourself

Leading a school is among the most demanding of jobs. Not only are teaching, learning, and healthy human development challenging activities to supervise and to manage, but to lead a whole community dedicated to these disciplines requires a sensitive human touch. In this culture, we expect the leaders of our schools to be practically superhuman. We want them to be accepting, understanding, patient, sensitive, capable of negotiating, and nurturing of both children and adults. Often for principals, the technical or management side of leadership demands entirely different talents than the human side (Cuban, 1988).

We cannot emphasize too strongly the importance of this human dimension to maintaining a healthy interpersonal climate in the school. For us, it is essential to the performance of both adults and children. The school's success as a community hinges on open communication channels, trust, and a degree of vulnerability among all its members. As principal, your own emotional condition and interpersonal relationships powerfully affect others' sense of the school's equilibrium and health. You are both a barometer of how things are going and a shaper of others' perceptions of how they are going (Whyte, 1994; Senge and others, 1994).

For this reason, we believe it is very important that principals listen to themselves—their feelings about colleagues, their sense of the tone in the building, and their gut evaluations. Just as listening to the school requires being open to information and feedback from the school, listening to yourself requires being open to your own feelings and intuitions about leading the school. This allows you to understand how your actions, expressions, and feelings are influencing others. It generates intrapersonal knowledge in the form of a "reality check" that lets you see yourself more clearly—and lets you know that you can trust yourself—as a leader.

Listening to yourself plays an even deeper role in shaping your trust in yourself as a school leader. The stresses of school leadership are likely to test even the most resolute self-believers not only because these stresses are so challenging but also because they are so numerous and unrelenting. Principals simply get worn down by the long hours, the emotional highs and lows, and the constant attention to people. Fatigue, overstimulation, blurred memories, and interpersonal questions lead many principals to wonder if the decisions they are making are wise. The conditions of your work can shake your trust in yourself as a leader.

Listening to yourself is an important way of determining if you have extended yourself beyond the limits of your own capacities. When you overextend yourself to the point that you doubt your ability to lead well, you are not apt to be serving your school as well as you can. It is time to reassess your role, your work, and yourself. In the next chapter, "Closing Letter: Caring for Yourself," we share some of our beliefs about the importance of your own personal and professional health to the personal and educational health of your school.

School leadership is a quest, not a battle to be won or a puzzle to be assembled. As with any quest, it calls for the companionship, resourcefulness, and energies of many talented people. Your challenge as a leader is to coalesce the capacities of your school community to meet the challenges of optimally educating and nurturing each child. Your greatest professional resource is that community itself. Successful principals learn to trust in that community and in its ability to respond healthfully to the challenges.

Your greatest personal asset, however, is to know yourself well enough to trust in yourself as a leader. Through your deepening understanding of the persisting tensions of schooling, of the talents and energies of those with whom you work, and of your own capacities, you will develop a sense of how and why you can trust in yourself. We believe that you develop this trust through experience and reflection.

Thankfully, successful educators, whether they be teachers, coaches, tutors, or community leaders, are engaged in this experience daily. They are learners and linkers. They operate from core values. They listen to their classrooms, their teams, their departments, their schools, their agencies. And increasingly, educators are learning the value of reflection—the key to listening to yourself. Through this book, we hope to encourage you to widen the circles of your caring and your influence to encompass the whole school community. Whether you are a principal or not, that community needs you to share in its leadership.

Closing Letter

Caring for Yourself

Dear Reader:

We began this book resolved to share with you an "elegantly simple" conception of the principalship: it is about working toward justice, developing fine teaching, integrating high achievement with wholesome personal qualities, promoting growth within the limits of your resources, changing practices while respecting everyone, creating collective ownership of and responsibility for kids' learning, and establishing the school as a community of autonomous, creative people. The seven persisting questions have painted for us a useful, albeit untidy, image of these core functions.

The questions, though, remind us that school leadership is a process, a working toward these qualities, a quest to do the best we can for our children, colleagues, and citizens. On that quest, we meet extraordinarily diverse demands for technical knowledge, demands that threaten to stretch our technical learning capacities beyond what any individual can singly possess. We have seen that leadership is a quest with and for people. It calls on two clusters of interpersonal capacities if the principal is to knit the diverse members of a school into a community of interest and effort (see Appendix B).

We suspect that, despite the "simplicity" of our seven questions, you have felt at times the hollow dread of being overwhelmed. You must have wondered, How can I be all these things to all these people? How can I know and do all I should? We now offer one final piece of advice: in the overwhelming yet invigorating world of school leadership, you cannot care for your school unless you also care for yourself.

Most principals feel overburdened by their jobs at one time or another, and some do continually. Indeed, you do not have a closed-ended job description. Everybody can—and does—place demands on you. You can become caught up in being everything to everybody all the time. The job can fulfill your own needs to be useful, to be a person of action, to feel like a leader. You can feel rewarded when you make the school run smoothly, when you have constant and varied contacts with people, and when you solve problems. The public exposure of the position, the feeling of being at the center of things, and the belief that you are shaping the education of children and the community can make the exhaustion and the long hours worthwhile.

The personal costs of working this way become painfully plain to most principals as well. The open-endedness of the job makes it extraordinarily easy to put in sixty or more hours at school in a typical week. Being responsive and helpful often leads to making phone calls from home at night or on weekends. Being at the center of things is physically taxing and, over long periods, is very stressful. Being important in the school and in the community can make the principal a target of resentment and a repository for public sentiments about schooling and other educational issues. These realities of principals' work threaten the boundaries of principals' lives: between public and private, between career and family, between professional and personal. Many of us need these boundaries to maintain a sense of balance and meaning in our lives. The leadership role and its work can readily consume us and our families.

We'll restate this dilemma in the form of our eighth—and most essential—persisting question: how can I attend well to my school's needs *and* to my own needs? Principals spend most of their time being other-centered. They are constantly helping others with their concerns: a child's worry about a lost hat, a late homework assignment, or a conflict at home; a parent's anxiety over discipline at home or a demanding teacher; a teacher's worry over limited supplies or how well the seventh-grade team is functioning; an assistant superintendent's need for budget data; a janitor's concern about kids hanging out in a remote corner of the school. The list is endless. And success begets success: the more you care and the more helpful you are, the longer stretches the line of problems to solve and people to help.

What does this do to principals? It places physical demands on them, fracturing their time and attention into many small pieces throughout the day. It extends the day into early morning and late evening and often into Saturdays and Sundays. Emotionally, it places them in personal and professional relationships with an expanding pool of people of all ages and persuasions. And it embroils principals in the aspirations, demands, and needs of these people—each one demanding that the leader make a choice, solve a problem, take action. Ultimately, these decisions produce ethical tensions, as different constituencies bring different values and aspirations to the school's table.

The work is not only physically exhausting. The constant choice making, done in close quarters with people whose hopes ride on which choices are made, is intellectually, emotionally, and psychically exhausting. It's very easy to lose sight of the whole picture and of your ability to fulfill your own expectations as a leader. These are the very moments when you run the risk of doing more harm than good to individuals, to groups, and to the school as a whole.

When and how do principals care for themselves during such exhausting work, so they can continue to care for their schools? Where's the time for the person inside the principal? When can principals be wives, husbands, mothers, fathers, sons, daughters, runners, fishermen, readers, hikers, jazz musicians, golfers, poetry writers, cooks, or any of the myriad identities that are important to personal health? When struggling to balance work and personal life, many principals ponder whether their own personal and family needs outweigh the needs of their school community. When does caring for myself, they wonder, supersede caring for others?

It is a question of epic proportions. All principals must make peace with it, even if it's on a temporary basis. We learn to say, "I'm not going to answer these four phone calls now because my children need me to be home tonight," or "I'm going to do this paperwork Friday because I'm so wiped out right now that I need to go swim at the Y." Such decisions require consciously determining a comfortable level for the priorities of your personal and professional lives.

That comfort level derives from a couple of factors that you can control. One is knowing your own limits, knowing when your caring for others and for the school is suffering because you are not caring for yourself. This is often thought of as a time-management problem, but it is really a work-management and self-management problem. Principals must be insightful enough about their work to know which parts are most vital to their leadership effectiveness. They must be insightful enough about their own performance to be able to sustain and focus their energies around these vital centers.

A second factor essential to establishing a healthy balance of professional and personal commitments is an understanding of what you and your family need for your lives to be fulfilling and healthy. What must be in place to keep vibrant your most important personal relationships and your sources of energy and love? To be clear about this requires self-understanding. Our intrapersonal knowledge must be sufficiently firm to permit us to say with confidence, "No, I will not do this for the school because I need to be at home or replenishing my wellsprings." Achieving this level of self-acceptance frees you to assert unashamedly some practical limits for yourself and the school.

Asserting limits based on your own or your family's needs does, of course, require interpersonal skill and sensitivity as well. It engages you in a sometimes delicate ethical dance between "to thine own self be true" and "am I my brother and sister's keeper?" As you weigh others' needs, demands, or proposals, you inevitably become concerned about how much those others feel cared for by you. Your choices often pit your definition of what is good against someone else's. As you prioritize options in order to make decisions, people will frequently interpret your actions as the principal's choice versus another person's or group's choice. Your role as a choice maker, though critically important, places you, the principal, in a lose-lose framework. If you do not act to change this situation, your leadership will be increasingly interpreted as being motivated mainly by your individual values and preferences, and everything you do will be perceived as being personally motivated. You will be held personally responsible for the consequences of all these choices.

This is very familiar territory for us and for most principals we know. A decision you've made with the purest of motives comes back to haunt you because those who didn't support the decision hold you responsible for its consequences. This is what wears principals down! This is what turns us against spiteful staff or community members, spiraling our relationships down into us-versus-them camps. This is what can lead principals to say, "What the hell, who cares anyway?" This sense of disappointment and despair eventually leads us to give up considering what others think or care about. When others don't seem to care for your choices, it's very tough to care about their choices or their reasoning—or even about them.

We haven't a neat prescription for this caring crisis. We do have two ideas for you to ponder. The first is that you can avoid the us-versus-them polarization that leads to lose-lose decisions by making sure that the school's values, not your own personal values, drive your choices. If you can develop a school community around a public vision of caring for children and a public value system for effective caring, the choices you make will neither be yours alone nor based on your own personal preferences. As we noted in Chapter Nine, you, together with the staff and community, will establish a value system, goals, and procedures for what all of you care about in your work.

The second idea to consider is that the school as a whole must share your caring crisis. Realistically, the school cannot carry out all proposals or meet all demands any more than you as the principal can. The school needs somebody who can help it winnow down its activities in order to protect the core it cares about most. We contend that this is one of your most profound functions, one that lies at the heart of your sense making as a principal. Fortunately, it is one in which your own personal needs coincide with the school's: you both need to focus your work around the vital centers that, collectively, you care about most deeply because neither you nor your school can be all things to all people all of the time.

We take great courage in this happy coincidence. In our view, school leaders need to treasure the complexity and the vibrancy of people trying to learn, to grow, to teach, and to thrive as a community. We have found the best way to do this is to view leadership as a quest to do our best for these people and these purposes. The quest is aptly shaped by persistent questions, questions that change in substance but not in form. The principal's most precious contribution is to help all the members of the school community make sense of their work as these questions surface and resurface.

Your anchor is a public vision of the school's commitment to children and public values for accomplishing that work. Keeping these foremost throughout the school community's activities keeps all of you in touch with what you care about. This gives meaning and direction to your daily work with children and with one another. And it all begins with caring for yourself.

Take care,
Becky, Gordy, and Richard

Appendix A
The International Network of Principals' Centers

The International Network of Principals' Centers is a ten-year-old collaboration of professional associations, informal practitioners' groups, universities, and education agencies working actively to strengthen leadership at the individual school level through professional development for leaders. The Network office is located within the Principals' Center at the Harvard Graduate School of Education. It has no full-time staff and is organized by an international advisory board of volunteer members.

The Network has a membership of principals' centers, academics, and practitioners in the United States and overseas. It is open to all groups and institutions committed to the growth of school leaders and the improvement of schools. The Network has to date functioned primarily as an information exchange and support system for member centers as they start up and attempt to sustain meaningful professional growth for school leaders, their schools, and their communities around the world.

The Network offers the following services to support school leaders:

- *The International Directory of Principals' Centers* features member centers with contact persons, descriptions of center activities, program references, and evaluation instruments.

- *The Annual Conversation* takes place every spring, when members meet for seminars, workshops, speakers, and discussions that continue to flow throughout the year.
- *Newsnotes*, the Network's quarterly newsletter, informs members of programs, conferences, workshops, and special interest items.
- *Reflections*, an annual journal, includes articles by principals, staff developers, university educators, and principals' center staff members.

For further information, please contact:

International Network of Principals' Centers
Harvard Graduate School of Education
336 Gutman Library
Cambridge, MA 02138
(617) 495–9812

Appendix B
A Framework for Assessing
Leadership Capacities

This appendix describes a useful framework for thinking about the capacities a principal draws upon as he or she leads. We suggest that you think of it as a way to assess yourself as a leader. It can help you to think about what leadership capacities are called for as principals deal with each of our seven tensions. It has helped us to frame our needs as leaders, to know what strengths to seek in others so as to complement our own strengths, and to establish professional development goals and activities.

The framework elaborates on the two domains of leadership knowledge we introduced in Chapter One: technical knowledge and beliefs about the learning, teaching, and organizing of schools; and interpersonal knowledge, skills, and qualities necessary to forge productive relationships with and among others. The technical domain consists of what you need to know about schools and schooling. This knowledge is necessary, but it is not sufficient by itself for you to be an effective leader. We believe it is the interpersonal domain that most shapes your eventual success at leading the school.

In Figure B.1, we present three central capacities for leadership, which we believe principals draw upon as they go about their work:

1. *A capacity to understand, to articulate and to draw upon a technical knowledge base* regarding (a) children's learning and

development, (b) teaching and other developmental activities, and (c) the organization of schooling experiences in an educative school environment. This capacity generally includes practical knowledge, theory, and research about effective learning, teaching, and school management and organization. It is essential to the leader's role in maintaining a school mission focused on children and learning and in making decisions that serve this mission.

2.   *A capacity to establish and sustain one-to-one working relationships* with students, parents, and especially professional colleagues. The major work principals do is face-to-face with other people. The principal's abilities to establish communication, trust, and mutual understanding come into play. Forming and sustaining one-to-one relationships with many individual students, educators, and citizens is essential to a principal's success as a positive influence for children's learning.

3.   *A capacity to facilitate the group activities necessary to developing healthy community norms* among students, staff, and citizens. Principals work with numerous groups that exist for various purposes: grade-level teams, student council, PTA, faculty, school board, sports teams, bands; the list is limitless. A principal's relationships and interactions with these groups shape his or her success at helping the whole school serve children and learning. In part, this happens through direct contact, and in part it occurs through symbolic actions—policies, decisions about the group's business, perceptions of the principal's values. A principal's capacity to facilitate effective group interactions determines the extent to which the school thinks, feels, and acts as a community; this in turn affects its ability to nurture children productively.

Figure B.1 cross-references these capacities with the goals expressed by each of the seven persisting questions. We find it helpful in identifying specific skills, knowledge, and personal qualities that principals might need in responding to the demands of each tension. We suggest you use the figure for discussion and reflection. It can assist in identifying professional development goals: are there skills or knowledge that you need to sharpen or to acquire in order to strengthen a capacity in some way?

The framework can help you identify these skills and qualities and lay the groundwork for professional growth. Although challenging, this kind of thinking is essential if a principal is to help his or her school community from becoming swamped in cross-purposes or divisive camps. We recommend for assistance Schön's *Reflective Practitioner* (1983), Osterman and Kottkamp's *Reflective Practice for Educators* (1993), Bridges's *Problem-Based Learning for Administrators* (1992), and Donaldson and Marnik's *Becoming Better Leaders* (1995).

We strongly recommend, as well, that you collaborate with a colleague or two in this activity. Each of you will view different aspects of the capacities and issues as significant; this diversity can expand your grasp of leadership requirements. More important, a trusted colleague can provide feedback from outside to help you assess your capacities and will be there to suggest resources for using this information wisely.

Here are some prompts for your self-assessment.

Reading down the columns, which of the persisting questions do I feel more knowledgeable about?

1. Is my knowledge more objective and research-based, or is it more subjective and experience-based?
2. How confident do I feel about these two types of knowledge? Am I confident enough to function effectively with others?

Reading across the rows, which of the three capacities do I feel most confident about?

1. Is my knowledge more objective or subjective in each capacity?
2. What evidence do I have that I can effectively draw upon each capacity as a whole?

Table B.1. Capacities for Handling Persisting Questions of School Leadership.

	Justice: To Treat All Children Justly	*Teaching: To Have All Teachers Be Effective Teachers*	*Purpose: To Balance Product and Process*
Capacity to use the knowledge base	Psychology of effective discipline What are appropriate school rules? What is a safe, healthy environment? What is "just" treatment?	Elements of effective teaching Identifying what needs to be taught Effective assessment of learning Assessment of teaching	Seeing multiple perspectives on the purposes of school Understanding my own philosophical values for school Assessing school success
Capacity to establish productive one-to-one relationships	Strategies for conflict management Establishing trust and open dialogue Clearly explaining reasons for treatment Responding to strong emotions	Effective supervision practices Motivating professional performance/growth Conferencing skills	Helping others expand their conception of purpose Patience, persistence Treating adults as you would have them treat students
Capacity to facilitate group thought and action	Building consistency among all adults Establishing a just school culture among adults How to model fair treatment among everyone	Creating schoolwide norms for good teaching Supporting risk taking and growth Collegial support and feedback systems	Establishing norms that value multiplicity Conducting meetings inclusively Encouraging ongoing discussions of ends *and* means

Resources: To Balance Needs and Resources	Change: To Push for Change and Respect the Status Quo	Ownership: To Balance Competing Adult Interests	Autonomy: To Respect Staff Autonomy and Preserve a Unified Effort
Prioritizing goals for students	Envisioning realistic improvement	Understanding community values	Understanding teacher-staff motivations
Identifying relevant resources	Strategies for systemic growth	Naming the differences among positions	Evaluating program impacts on children
Knowing planning processes	Evaluation of performance	Political, social, and cultural influences on views on school	Translating student needs into curriculum
	Processes of adult learning and performance change		
Using mediation processes	Setting individual expectations for professional improvement	Two-way communication with a variety of citizens	Mediation process
Communicating clearly	Assuring individuals of their value	Boundary setting (within our mission)	Conflict management
Being realistic yet optimistic	Stimulating creativity	Mediation skills	Goal setting and performance evaluation
Stimulating resourcefulness			Matching jobs with people's talents
Involving others in planning	Setting collective expectations for improvement	Communicating respect of all communities	Establishing norms for respectful disagreement
Celebrating success	Valuing others while challenging their practices	Molding consensus for core goals and operating principles	Leading staff assessment of curriculum relevance and impacts
Setting ambitions yet attainable goals		Celebrating diversity within limits	
Creating a "we can" attitude			

Note: Many entries may apply to other columns as well.

3. Can I draw upon each capacity to help us understand a challenge we face and take action to address it?

Using these assessments, ask yourself:

1. What are my strong points? What personal and professional resources can I draw upon?

2. What are my challenges? What resources can I draw upon to begin to meet them?

References

Acheson, K. A., and Gall, M. D. *Techniques in the Clinical Supervision of Teachers: Preservice and Inservice Applications.* White Plains, N.Y.: Longman, 1980.

Ackerman, R., Donaldson, G. A., Jr., Simpson, G., and van der Bogert, R. "Reflections." *Journal of the International Network of Principals' Centers,* Cambridge, Mass.: Harvard University, 1984–95.

Apple, M. W. *Ideology and Curriculum.* (2nd ed.) New York: Routledge & Kegan Paul, 1990.

Argyris, C., and Schön, D. A. *Theory in Practice: Increasing Professional Effectiveness.* San Francisco: Jossey-Bass, 1974.

Association for Supervision and Curriculum Development. *Moral Education in the Life of the School: A Report from the ASCD Panel on Moral Education.* Alexandria, Va.: Association for Supervision and Curriculum Development, 1988.

Barth, R. S. *Improving Schools from Within: Teachers, Parents, and Principals Can Make the Difference.* Jossey-Bass Education Series. San Francisco: Jossey-Bass, 1990.

Bennis, W., and Nanus, B. *Leaders: The Strategies for Taking Charge.* New York: HarperCollins, 1985.

Berlin, I. (1990). *The Crooked Timber of Humanity: Chapters in the History of Ideas.* New York: Knopf.

Blase, J., and Kirby, P. C. *Bringing Out the Best in Teachers: What Effective Principals Do.* Newbury Park, Calif.: Corwin Press, 1992.

Block, P. *Stewardship: Choosing Service over Self-Interest.* San Francisco: Berrett-Koehler, 1993.

Bolman, L., and Deal, T. E. *Becoming a Teacher Leader: From Isolation to Collaboration.* Newbury Park, Calif.: Corwin Press, 1993.

Bridges, E. M. *The Incompetent Teacher: The Challenge and the Response.* Stanford Series on Education and Public Policy. Washington, D.C.: Falmer Press, 1986.

Bridges, E. M. *Problem-Based Learning for Administrators.* Eugene, Oreg.: Education Resources Information Center, 1992.

Carmichael, L. B. *McDonogh 15: Becoming a School*. New York: Avon Books, 1981.

Coles, R. *The Moral Life of Children*. Boston: Atlantic Monthly Press, 1986.

Covaleskie, J. F. "Discipline and Morality: Beyond Rules and Consequences." *Educational Forum*, 1992, 56(2).

Covey, S. *First Things First: To Live, to Love, to Learn, to Leave a Legacy*. New York: Simon & Schuster, 1994.

Cremin, L. A. *The Transformation of the School: Progressivism in American Education, 1876–1957*. New York: Vintage Books, 1961.

Cuban, L. *The Managerial Imperative and the Practice of Leadership in Schools*. Albany: State University of New York Press, 1988.

Cunningham, W. G., and Gresso, D. W. *Cultural Leadership: The Culture of Excellence in Education*. Needham Heights, Mass.: Allyn & Bacon, 1993.

Dewey, J. *The School and Society*. (rev. ed.) Chicago: University of Chicago Press, 1915.

Dewey, J. *Experience in Education*. Kappa Delta Pi, Lecture Series, New York: Macmillan, 1950.

Donaldson, G. A., Jr. *Learning to Lead: The Dynamics of the High School Principalship*. Contributions to the Study of Education, no. 45. Westport, Conn.: Greenwood Press, 1991.

Donaldson, G. A., Jr., and Marnik, G. (eds.). *As Leaders Learn: Personal Stories of Growth in School Leadership*. Newbury Park, Calif.: Corwin Press, 1995a.

Donaldson, G. A., Jr., and Marnik, G. *Becoming Better Leaders: The Challenge of Improving Student Learning*. Newbury Park, Calif.: Corwin Press, 1995b.

Duke, D. L. *School Leadership and Instructional Improvement*. New York: Random House, 1987.

Fullan, M. G. *The New Meaning of Educational Change*. (2nd ed.) New York: Teachers College Press, 1993.

Fullan, M. G., and Hargreaves, A. *What's Worth Fighting For? Working Together for Your School*. Andover, Mass.: Regional Laboratory for Educational Improvement of the Northeast and Islands; Toronto: Ontario Public School Teachers' Federation, 1991.

Glatthorn, A. A. *Differentiated Supervision*. Alexandria, Va.: Association for Supervision and Curriculum Development, 1984.

Glickman, C. D. *Supervision of Instruction: A Developmental Approach*. Needham, Mass.: Allyn & Bacon, 1985.

Glickman, C. D. (ed.). *Supervision in Transition*. 1992 Yearbook of the Association for Supervision and Curriculum Development. Alexandria, Va.: Association for Supervision and Curriculum Development, 1992.

Goodlad, J. L. *A Place Called School: Prospects for the Future*. New York: McGraw-Hill, 1984.

Greenfield, W. "Research on Public School Principals: A Review and Recommendations." Paper prepared for the National Conference on the Principalship convened by the National Institute of Education, 1982.

Gutmann, A. *Democratic Education*. Princeton, N.J.: Princeton University Press, 1987.

Hebert, B. "Portfolios Invite Reflection—from Students and Staff." *Educational Leadership*. Association for Supervision and Curriculum Development May, 1992.

Heifetz, R. A. *Leadership Without Easy Answers*. Cambridge, Mass.: Belknap Press of Harvard University Press, 1994.

Heifetz, R. A., and Sinder, R. "Managing the Public's Problem-Solving." In R. B. Reich (ed.), *The Power of Public Ideas*. Cambridge, Mass.: Ballinger, 1988.

Jentz, B. C., and Wofford, J. W. *Leadership and Learning: Personal Change in a Professional Setting*. New York: McGraw-Hill, 1979.

Johnson, S. M. *Teachers at Work: Achieving Success in Our Schools*. New York: Basic Books, 1990.

Joyce, B. R. (ed.). *Changing School Culture Through Staff Development*. 1990 Yearbook of the Association for Supervision and Curriculum Development. Alexandria, Va.: Association for Supervision and Curriculum Development, 1990.

Joyce, B. R., and Showers, B. *Student Achievement Through Staff Development: Fundamentals of School*. (2nd ed.) White Plains, N.Y.: Longman, 1995.

Kallick, B. "Changing Schools into Communities for Thinking," North Dakota Study Group Monograph, 1989.

Kohlberg, L. *Essays on Moral Development*. San Francisco: HarperSanFrancisco, 1981.

Leithwood, K. A. (1990). "The Principal's Role in Teacher Development," in Joyce, Bruce R. *Changing School Culture Through Staff Development*. ASCD Yearbook, Alexandria, Va.

Levine, S. L. *Promoting Adult Growth in Schools: The Promise of Professional Development*. Needham Heights, Mass.: Allyn & Bacon, 1989.

Lieberman, A. (ed.). *Building a Professional Culture in Schools*. Professional Development and Practice Series. New York: Teachers College Press, 1988.

Little, J. W. "Norms of Collegiality and Experimentation: Workplace Conditions of School Success." *American Educational Research Journal*, 1982, *19*, 325–340.

Little, J. W., and McLaughlin, M. W. (eds.). *Teachers' Work: Individuals, Colleagues, and Contexts*. Professional Development and Practice Series. New York: Teachers College Press, 1993.

McGreal, T. L. *Successful Teacher Evaluation*. Alexandria, Va.: Association for Supervision and Curriculum Development, 1983.

McNeil, L. M. *Contradictions of Control: School Structure and School Knowledge*. New York: Routledge & Kegan Paul, 1986.

McPherson, R. B., Crowson, R. L., and Pitner, N. J. *Managing Uncertainty: Administrative Theory and Practice in Education.* Columbus, Ohio: Merrill, 1986.

Maeroff, G. *The Empowerment of Teachers: Overcoming the Crisis of Confidence.* New York: Teachers College Press, 1988.

Milstein, M. M. *Restructuring Schools: Doing It Right—Roadmaps to Success.* Newbury Park, Calif.: Corwin Press, 1993.

Muncey, D. E., and McQuillan, P. J. "Preliminary Findings from a Five-Year Study of the Coalition of Essential Schools." *Phi Delta Kappan,* 1993, *74,* 486–489.

Murphy, J. T. "The Unheroic Side of Leadership: Notes from the Swamp." *Phi Delta Kappan,* 1988, *69,* 654–659.

National Commission on Excellence in Education. *A Nation at Risk: The Imperative for Educational Reform.* Washington, D.C.: U.S. Department of Education, 1983.

Noddings, N. *Caring: A Feminine Approach to Ethics and Moral Education.* Berkeley: University of California Press, 1984.

Osterman, K. F., and Kottkamp, R. B. *Reflective Practice for Educators: Improving Schooling Through Professional Development.* Newbury Park, Calif.: Corwin Press, 1993.

Patterson, J. L., Purkey, S. C., and Parker, J. V. *Productive School Systems for a Nonrational World.* Alexandria, Va.: Association for Supervision and Curriculum Development, 1986.

Rosenholtz, S. *Teachers' Workplace: The Social Organization of Schools.* White Plains, N.Y.: Longman, 1989.

Rost, J. C. *Leadership for the Twenty-First Century.* New York: Praeger, 1991.

Saphier, J. *How to Make Supervision and Evaluation Really Work: Supervision and Evaluation in the Context of Strengthening School Culture.* Carlisle, Mass.: Research for Better Teaching, 1993.

Saphier, J., Bigda-Peyton, T., and Pierson, G. *How to Make Decisions That Stay Made.* Alexandria, Va.: Association for Supervision and Curriculum Development, 1989.

Saphier, J., and D'Auria, J. *How to Bring Vision to School Improvement Through Core Outcomes, Commitments and Beliefs.* Carlisle, Mass.: Research for Better Teaching, 1993.

Saphier, J., and Gower, R. *The Skillful Teacher: Building Your Teaching Skills.* Carlisle, Mass.: Research for Better Teaching, 1987.

Schön, D. A. *The Reflective Practitioner: How Professionals Think in Action.* New York: Basic Books, 1983.

Senge, P. M. *The Fifth Discipline: The Art and Practice of the Learning Organization.* New York: Doubleday, 1990a.

Senge, P. M. "The Leader's New Work: Building Learning Organizations." *Sloan Management Review,* 1990b.

Senge, P. M., and others. *The Fifth Discipline Fieldbook: Strategies and Tools for Building a Learning Organization.* New York: Doubleday, 1994.

Sergiovanni, T. J. *Moral Leadership: Getting to the Heart of School Improvement.* Jossey-Bass Education Series. San Francisco: Jossey-Bass, 1992.

Sizer, T. R. *Horace's Compromise: The Dilemma of the American High School.* Boston: Houghton Mifflin, 1984.

Smith, W. F., and Andrews, R. L. *Instructional Leadership: How Principals Make a Difference.* Alexandria, Va.: Association for Supervision and Curriculum Development, 1989.

Sockett, H. *The Moral Base for Teacher Professionalism.* Professional Ethics in Education Series. New York: Teachers College Press, 1993.

Stanley, S. J., and Popham, W. J. (eds.). *Teacher Evaluation: Six Prescriptions for Success.* Alexandria, Va.: Association for Supervision and Curriculum Development, 1988.

Strike, K. A., and Soltis, J. F. *The Ethics of Teaching.* (2nd ed.) Thinking About Education Series. New York: Teachers College Press, 1992.

Troen, V. & Boles, K. "Two Teachers Examine the Power of Teacher Leadership." In D. R. Walling (ed.), *Teachers As Leaders: Perspectives on the Professional Development of Teachers,* (pp. 275–296). Phi Delta Kappa Educational Foundation, Bloomington, Ind., 1994.

Tyack, D. B. *The One Best System: A History of American Urban Education.* Cambridge, Mass.: Harvard University Press, 1974.

Tyack, D. B., and Hansot, E. *Learning Together: A History of Coeducation in American Schools.* New Haven, Conn.: Yale University Press; New York: Russell Sage Foundation, 1990.

Wheatley, M. *Leadership and the New Science: Learning About Organization from an Orderly Universe.* San Francisco: Berrett-Koehler, 1992.

Whyte, D. *The Heart Aroused: Poetry and the Preservation of the Soul in Corporate America.* New York: Doubleday, 1994.

Index